Sofa

Plays for strong, older, female actors
who want to get off the couch!

Pam Calabrese MacLean

© 2021 Pam Calabrese MacLean

All rights reserved. No part of this book may be reproduced or transmitted in any form or by any means, electronic or mechanical, including photocopying, or by any information storage or retrieval system, without permission in writing from the publisher.

Cover image: Elizabeth Marie Caslake

Editor: Andrew Wetmore

ISBN: 978-1-990187-23-0
First edition November, 2021

2475 Perotte Road
Annapolis County, NS
B0S 1A0

moosehousepress.com
info@moosehousepress.com

We live and work in Mi'kma'ki, the ancestral and unceded territory of the Mi'kmaw people. This territory is covered by the "Treaties of Peace and Friendship" which Mi'kmaw and Wolastoqiyik (Maliseet) people first signed with the British Crown in 1725. The treaties did not deal with surrender of lands and resources but in fact recognized Mi'kmaq and Wolastoqiyik (Maliseet) title and established the rules for what was to be an ongoing relationship between nations. We are all Treaty people.

Performance rights

The copyright for the plays in this book belongs to the author. In buying this book you get the enjoyment of putting on the plays in the theatre inside your head, as you read them.

If you want to perform these scripts in any way, including as staged readings for a non-paying audience, as an audio play, or as an amateur or professional live or recorded production, you **must** obtain permission in writing from the author or their representative. To do otherwise is a violation of copyright and not a nice thing to do to another theatre person.

For information about royalties and obtaining performance rights, send an email to info@moosehousepress.com. We will forward serious inquiries to the author.

"Sunnyside Café" first appeared in *One for the Road: New Plays for one actor*. Winnipeg: Signature Editions, edited by Kit Brennan, 2012. www.signature-editions.com

Also by Pam Calabrese MacLean

Poetry

The Dead Can't Dance. Ronsdale Press, 2009
ISBN 9781553800699

Twenty-Four Names For Mother. The Paper Journey Press, 2006
ISBN 0977315622

Children's books

A Christmas Crisis. Hamboyan Publishing, 1989
ISBN 0921882017

The Gift. Hamboyan Publishing, 1988.
ISBN 0921882009

Other

Flavour of Varmland (co-editor/translator). Varmland Museum, Sweden, 2006.

Taking a seat on the *Sofa*

Pam Calabrese MacLean has been a go-go dancer in Montreal, a drug-crisis worker, and a salesperson for hearing aids. She lived on a farm along with horses, cows, pigs, chickens, ducks, rabbits, and a skunk in the pantry. On the night of a full moon, she once rode her horse bareback, while naked, at Dunn's Beach. In other words, she is fearless.

Her plays are about people who could live next door, revealing their pain, their joys, and their desires. Two women wait for a bus, but it's not a bus trip they take: it's a journey through clouded memories that's both improbable and true. A dead woman talks to a woman who is alive, and they form a secret alliance. A man takes his wife peppermints in the nursing home as a way of trying to bring her back to him.

What makes these plays so poignant? There is a moment in "Her Father's Barn," a play that gives us the unforgettable Ida-Mae, when a mother's grief is held, illuminated. This is one of the lit candles of Calabrese MacLean's poetry, tucked into a play that is about the many-sided life of a woman who has spread her love widely. The vividness of the language in this play, as in the others, is what haunts us after it's over. Yet lyricism is only one strand of the whole: the stories told on *Sofa*'s stage have poetry, yes, but they're also funny.

This makes for the wonderfully changeable weather of all the plays. In "Is it Wednesday?" two women are bewildered and forgetful, then comical, then deeply insightful, then bewildered and forgetful. As the audience, we think we know what this play is about, but these two characters, Mavis and Stella, tilt the playing field so often that we get bewildered too. Still, they show us how to walk into a world of shadows with nonchalance and wit. They show us how to be fearless. And this, above all, is the marvel of the plays in *Sofa*.

Anne Simpson, author of *Speechless*

Then it happened

All dressed for International Women's Day, I was sporting my Calvin Klein socks, hoping by the time I got there I would look, even a little, like the woman in CK's ads. Or the guy!

I misdialed the number of the friend who was to drive me and a strange voice answered. Strange yet familiar. We talked for an hour. She was changing her bed. She was waiting for her daughter who visits every Saturday evening. She was very excited when I explained IWD to her.

I can hear her voice whenever I want.

As a child I talked in different voices most of the time. Mom would always scold me, but when I overheard Mom telling Dad that I needed a psychiatrist I went back to my own voice. I didn't know what a psychiatrist was but I was pretty sure it was not good.

Unwittingly I began stockpiling voices!

By the time I finished growing up, getting married, having a family, I'd forgotten all about the voices. I started my writing career with children's books because someone told me they were easy. NOT!

Also I had a captive audience in my three sons. I published two kids' books before I went off to a week-long writing workshop only to be told that my writing, while good, was too dark for kids.

So I moved on to adults! And poetry. I didn't like poems at first but they were shorter than novels, easier to find time for them. Kind of true but not so much as I'd hoped. I spent a few years writing exceedingly bad poetry. I was the only one my words touched. And they depressed me.

Then it happened: I heard my Dad's voice, although his words were garbled, the feelings were clear. I wrote a good poem about my Dad's six eyes. I published many poems inspired by my Dad and published two volumes of poetry: *Paper Journey Press* and *Ronsdale*.

Not every poem had a companion voice stirring up the dust in my brain, but Ida-Mae spoke loudly. I wrote a series of poems from my point of view about this fictional rural Nova Scotia woman. I presented 'The Ida-Mae Poems' at a one-act-play festival in Antigonish, where it's said if there's a poet in the festival, they didn't get enough plays.

Pauline, the meekest *tour de force* I'd ever met, approached me after the evening, suggesting that The Ida-Mae poems would make a wonderful monologue. So it began: a wonderful friendship; an award winning play (also an award winning Ida-Mae) and a transition from poet to playwright.

One of the challenges was the switch from third person to first person. Not just a matter of exchanging pronouns. It had to be a totally changed outlook on everything. I knew what I knew about Ida-Mae but I also needed to let go of my voice, my wit, so I could hear hers. By the time "Her Father's Barn" was ready to fly, I had two perspectives on the day-to-day things I saw, heard and felt: mine and Ida-Mae's.

All my plays start with a voice. Sometimes a voice has a story to tell. Other times I have to tease the story out of the voice. A little like removing burdocks from a horse's mane.

At the same time as I was learning plays and actors and staging and all, I was also paying attention to the mature women actors who felt that there were few strong parts for the aging female. I made a deal with myself that I would try to fill the gap. And to some extent I feel I have. Reviewing the plays for publication was a second chance to scrutinize the plays, unplump the cushions on the sofa and get Strong Older Female Actors on their feet again.

PCM
November, 2021

For my dear friend Pauline,
Who owns every stage
And a huge chunk of my heart.

The author has created the characters, conversations, interactions, and events of these plays; and any resemblance of any character to any real person is coincidental.

Contents

Performance rights...3
Taking a seat on the *Sofa*..5
Then it happened...7
Cast requirements and run times..12
Her Father's Barn..13
    From page to stage: "Her Father's Barn"..33
    "Her Father's Barn" production history:...34
    Ida-Mae—from poem to play..35
Janitor...39
    The Seeds for "Janitor"..57
Is it Wednesday?...59
    A bench is a bench is a bench..73
Peppermints...75
    The inspiration for "Peppermints"..89
Awake...91
    About "Awake"..107
Wanna Bet?...109
    About "Wanna bet?"...135
Who Knew?...137
    A running joke..155
Sunnyside Café..157
    Thoughts on "Sunnyside Café"..177
    In the shadow of Sunnyside Café..179
    Acknowledgements..181
    About the author..183

Pam Calabrese MacLean

Cast requirements and run times

Her Father's Barn – 59 minutes
One woman in her mid-70s

Janitor – 15 minutes
One older woman
One man in his 20s

Is it Wednesday? - 10 minutes
Two older women

Peppermints – 15 minutes
One older woman
One older man
Intercom voice

Awake – 10 minutes
Two older women
Delivery man voice

Wanna Bet? - 15 minutes
One woman around 80
One woman in her 50s

Who Knew? - 15 minutes
Two older women

Sunnyside Café – 45 minutes
One woman in her fifties

Her Father's Barn

Time
Now.

Setting
The interior of a barn. There should be the indication of a corral, in which there is an unseen cow. A bale of straw is available as a seat and the floor is covered in straw and hay sweepings. A broom and pitchfork are in evidence, as are several old pieces of clothing and such gear as a barn would have.
   The lighting should give the impression of a single hanging light.

Cast

Ida-Mae, a woman in her mid-70s

Pam Calabrese MacLean

Her Father's Barn

We are in a barn, in darkness. Any pre-show MUSIC fades out. IDA-MAE enters USR, muttering to herself. She feels along the barn wall, then slaps the light switch.
LIGHTS UP.

IDA-MAE
Now we're both awake!
    Imagine the hospital calling me from my bed to tell me Angus had the queerest dream. Says I'd better check the cow. Sixty years of Angus and his queer dreams. And most likely himself back asleep, some pretty young nurse, holdin' his hand, before I was into my winter boots. Well how are ya now, cow? That'd be Angus's line.
    How are ya now, Ida-Mae? He was always saying that to me. Used it like a 'pay attention, woman' at the beginning of whatever. And again at the end to let me know he's done. Real bad in the bedroom where he'd announce his lust with a 'HOWAREYANOW?' and before I could answer he'd be asking again.
    I remember the first time I really looked at Angus. I was just after tellin' old Maud Purcell in the strictest of confidence, which is no doubt the self-same way that she told every living soul in and about Benign Harbour, I was just after tellin' her how I was wantin' to marry a loose-tongued, long-fingered, city man. No snub-nosed, blunt-fingered, country bumpkin was ever gonna rub me the wrong way.
    In the end I did choose a bumpkin. Angus MacHine. Most all the men and boys was off fighting the war. Our choices whittled down to three. There was Willy The Chicken Benoit—fine looking boy, brain of a chicken. Lawrence Cecil MacDowell—he was just plain scary. Something about his eyes put me in mind of my father.
    And then there was Angus. The girls looked on the army not

wanting Angus and his flat feet as somewhat of a blessing. He could've walked down the wharf road with any one of them.
　He wanted me.
　I can't say I thought anything about Angus was a blessing at all but then one night we was up behind the old legion playing in the long summer grass and he did something clever with them blunt fingers of his and I thought maybe I'd been wrong about other things too. And the boy had a grand nose.
　Ya did know, Gladie? What a name for a cow!

　SOUND: Cow mooing

IDA-MAE
Yeah. Ya did know that the size of a man's nose lets you know ahead, the size of his bus-in-ness. Kind of a forerunner. And no one minds a girl staring at a fella's face!
　Course years of my good cooking and rich Guernsey cream, Angus's nose hardly shows up at all anymore. Hasn't caused a stir in a bit.
　Can't say I was anxious to marry. Getting pregnant changed that. Summer of 1945, Angus played the fiddle at our wedding, and I danced the night to his tune. Hot, sticky, wet and tired. Dreamin' of kissin' off the last guest. Every break in the music, Angus got to go outside to cool off. Fearsome hot Ida-Mae he'd say giving me the big wink. Somewhere around 'bout the third wink the thought of leavin' Angus flitted through me mind—quick as a spring rabbit. I just laughed at myself—I heard a one woman who ran from the altar and more that wished to God they had but I'd not ever heard of runnin' from the dance.
　I felt the baby move once but only once after we was joined. I woke one morning, no baby. Doc Clayton said highsterical pregnancy. He was right. About the highsteria anyway. Angus mostly.
　God, I feared a lifetime of it. Highsteria and Angus calling the tune. He did have most to do with hot, sticky, wet and tired and nothing, nothing save the fiddling, to do with the first eight of my

Sofa

nine children.

Things changed 'tween me and Angus after that strange pregnancy. Oh, he still wanted me once a day, regular as shaving, but he'd started spending most of his time in this barn.

I try to forget that this was my father's barn. Me and me five brothers grew up here. Every Saturday morning in summer, Ma would drag the big tub from the barn, set it to the side of the double doors and fill it from the old well. That water would warm all day and by evening the six of us would huddle naked, waiting on our turn.

Twelve years gawking at me brothers before I realized there was nothing wrong with me. But I wasn't 13 'fore I knew how I'd been blessed by what I didn't have.

My father stood quiet in that doorway, every bath night.

Mostly I came out here with Ma. Something special about warm eggs and the smells of hay and birth and new milk. I was always asking why the fathers were kept to themselves. My Ma'd smile so sad.

The first time I remember men in this barn, there were five of them, hard and hurried. Come to help with a birthing. They sweated, grunted, pulled till that calf lay, warm and dead, at their feet. I screamed Bastards! and me father slapped me again and again and again.

After that I came to the barn, secret. Late at night. I'd watch and listen, safe. Me father ruined that too. Caught me here. Held me down. Drove off all me senses with his own. Tore me second to best dress.

Afterwards, I'd thought about driving the pitchfork into my own leg, a hurt anyone could plainly see. Crying out and blaming him. But I didn't do it. Didn't do nothing. Didn't even tell Ma. I guessed she already knew about men, and wounds that never come to scars.

When Angus and I moved here, I'd still have nothing to do with this barn. I never told Angus what me Father'd done to me and he tried all kinds of foolishness to get me in here. One time he hid my birthday present in the mow and he was forever callin' me in to help him with some job he'd already bragged about finishing the day before. Once he even pretended he'd sprained his ankle. Callin' out for help. Ida-Mae, come in here. I need ya. I think I busted me leg. But I looked in the window first and there was himself standin' atop two bales a hay lookin' out the self-same window. I'd a gone in and strangled him 'cept I'd scared him so bad he toppled off them bales and nearly did hisself in!

It was the old cat got me in here in the end. I'd had her most all my life. Angus said she was holed up in the barn. Same spot for two days. Afraid he'd scare her off so it had to be me go in. "She gonna die, Ida-Mae," And I yelled at him, "Angus MacHine there are worse places to be than dead."

He saw me cross myself and spit before I stepped through that door but he didn't hear me swear it'd be the last time. Good he didn't 'cos once I got inside, I knew right off how hard Angus was trying to make this barn his own. He'd opened it up, let in more light. Seemed like he must of figured it hisself 'cos he'd started sweeping and kept on 'til my father was out that door like dirt. I wanted to believe. But what I knew was somethin' else. Didn't have the heart then, don't have the heart now to tell Angus, it had to be me graspin' that broom, had to be me doing the sweepin', has to me...

The old cat had lost a leg and her due to birth any day. She'd neither eat nor drink. The vet said get rid of them kittens, but Angus said that'd be the worst thing—for me or the cat, I was never sure—so I spent day and night in this barn until them kittens came and that old cat remembered something other than dying.

Angus was real happy having me and the cat in the barn with him and his cows. But that brood was making me real anxious for a family of my own.

Six years I'd been married to Angus and his I'm-gonna-do-this-no-matter-what-lust and I was barren, real fidgety and bored enough to be over-listening to Maud Purcell and Bernice Bates on the phone. Maud was saying, always saying something, that one, "If ya can't get a mare in foal—change the stud".

I yelled, "YIPPEE," slammed the phone and did a little dance.

My first child, Maud-Bernice, was born nine months later, give or take the few days it took me to find the perfect stud. And that is how I think about Maud-Bernice's dad. Perfect stud.

In the end I needed pet names for all me lovers. Help keep straight who belonged to who. On each child's birthday I spend time remembering the father. I still chuckle over Catherine-Billy's dad. Nick-named him 'Bungalow Bill', nothing upstairs but, Lord, the basement.

Surprises me I got to like sex at all. After my father. I wasn't supposed to. Not accordin' to everything I read. Ya see, Gladie, I was spendin' a lot a time in Doc Clayton's office. Mostly waitin' on him to tell me I was pregnant again. Bert was my second to last baby and with him I waited till I was nearly seven months gone. Doc Clayton says to me, "What were ya thinkin', waitin' so long, Ida-Mae?" "I was thinkin' I was pregnant. Just like every other time."

Well I shouldn't a been so cocky 'cos a few years later I had Emma figured for the change.

But I was talkin' about the magazines in the doctor's office and how it seemed in every one some women or another was tellin' what her uncle or her father or her grandfather had done to her. And all them women had no end of troubles and most had to do with sex. I might have given up sex in the beginning but I wanted babies that bad.

But it was more than that. Angus felt safe. Right from that first time up behind the legion with him all fumblin' and gentle it was easy to believe this was nothin' like my father.

Them days I could tell myself a lie if it let me get on with what I wanted.

Once we was wed and he thought he could have me anytime he wanted, he sort a settled. Always the same time. Always the same place. Got so he'd put his hand on my shoulder in a certain way and I knew what was comin'. And what was next.

Angus, sex-by-number MacHine! Many's the time I did the shoppin' list in my head while Angus was working his way from nine to ten. Then he'd be asking real quiet, "How are ya now, Ida-Mae?" And then snorin'. More than once I wished his love-makin' could get me movin' like his snorin'!

I wonder Gladie, can you owe a debt for somethin' done to ya?

That's the closest I can come to sayin what I felt about havin' babies. Like I owed somethin'. Like there was somethin' that needed doin' better. Doin' right.

And I got my babies.

Likin' sex was just the butter on the broccoli.

SOUND: cow mooing.

IDA-MAE
Molasses on the oats, Gladie! Molasses on the oats!

Oh, I tried a couple of times to tell Angus what would make me happy in bed, but he told me that men know that kind of thing naturally, and he didn't want to be the one to ruin things, trying something new. "No siree, not me, Ida-Mae."

There's plenty I'd like to talk to Angus about.

SOUND: cow mooing

IDA-MAE
Cows for one. I don't have to tell you how much Angus loves cows. Respects their natural goodness, he says. I'd like to know Gladie, when ever you been tempted.

Saved my hide once, Angus's respect for cows. You see, back then Angus grew zucchini and I was the one got to drive around town trying to give the stuff away. But the townies were getting smarter. Locking their cars in the fall, to keep them from filling up with Angus's zucchini. I was about to give up and head home, when I spotted a prairie licence plate.

That car was fire-engine red and the doors O P E N.

I got caught by Red-Hughie, his hair matched his car. City boy, not too familiar with zucchini. Managed to give him the whole load and in return he gave Angus a second son.

I must've been a little bit in love that time. Didn't really think it through. Didn't even try to match Red-Hughie's features with the features of the fathers of Angus's other children. Never once figured on William-Xavier being born with his head on fire and freckles.

Good thing for me Angus's prize cow had done the same thing year before: produced a calf the colour of which Angus couldn't figger. I knew the neighbour's bull was what happened. But in Angus's heart that cow was above suspicion and on the strength of her strange calf, so was I.

My last child, Emma-Lucille, was no strange calf. She was the dead spit of Angus, and his only flesh and blood child. The only one Angus loved more than his cows. He didn't know why Emma-Lucille was different, just that somehow she was. There was nothing Emma couldn't convince Angus to do. The day she made him into a scarecrow. Stuffed his shirt with straw. Up his pant legs and under his hat. Angus itched in the worst way for weeks.

I can hear Emma's laugh. And Angus's right over top of it like he had no choice. Which he never did with Emma.

She'd a spent every waking minute in this barn with Angus. Watchin' him. Followin'. Mimicin'. Ah, God, she could swagger just like Angus. And he never did turn round fast enough to catch her. Not that he ever minded. Not what Emma did least ways.

Many the nights I came out here lookin'. Angus late from chores. The others gone from the table. No Angus. No Emma. I kept thinkin' I believed in Angus, but then it'd me being my ma and not lookin', not wantin' to see what was right there plain. Not wantin' to know. And I'd be out the door. Runnin' out here to this barn. I never made the trip without the taste of my father in my mouth.

And I swear I loved Angus that first night I burst through the barn door to find himself leaning against the stall, watchin' Emma where she'd fallen asleep.

Oh he knew what I was thinkin' all right, but he just beckoned me with his head. "Look at her, Ida-Mae. Look at her." And himself turnin' away fast so I couldn't see how hard he loved her.

It should'a been enough.

Angus had a special way of lookin' at Emma right from the day he saw her born.

The only one of the children he did see born. Oh Gladie, I'm not likely to forget that day. It was the young doctor's first birthing. He couldn't stop staring at the delivery site and Angus's eyeballs were rolling madly around the room, desperate to look anywhere else. He accidentally looks at me, my big feet hanging in the air. I lift my head, between my own legs and shout, "It'd be good one of ya took yer hands out of yer pockets and got ready to catch."

Angus was backing toward the delivery room door when Emma-Lucille spilled into the room. Angus caught her. Settled easy. I held the sight of them, clear and sharp. Saw all that Angus had let go. And for a minute, I almost forgave him my mistakes.

Emma was always surprising me. Even before she was born. Me and my friend Lucy had gone to the quiltin'. Trying to be regular, Lucy called it. There was a lot a talk the like of which I'd never heard discussed before. Men and sex, birthin' and such. Mostly the young ones talkin' and the old ones lookin' like every word was stitchin' their mouths shut tighter and tighter.

All that talk was makin' me feel brave so on the walk home I said to Lucy that I thought me monthly troubles was at an end, but wasn't it funny I said, I didn't think the change was supposed to feel like being pregnant.

Lucy laughed most all the way home. That was the Christmas before Emma was born. And I'd not had a lover for 2 years and I was pretty sure Angus was fishin' without a hook. I could scarce believe it pregnant at my age and with me husband's child.

And everyday I thought more and more about that first child. The one we wed for. The one that changed her mind. Disappeared into nothing. I thought maybe me and Angus were being given back what we'd lost.

Fool I was then to think I knew loss.

Me friend Lucy knew loss. Three boys. Two girls. Gone. She said what nearly killed her was her body tryin' to make room. Tryin' to take them all back. Said her heart had to go.

I couldn't really tell what she meant until after Emma.

Sofa

    Remembering Emma-Lucille is like breathing. Week or so back, I was braiding sweet-grass and real sudden it was Emma's hair. Just that same shade of dust and full of the north wind.
    I braided it every morning, Emma wriggling under my fingers. And those braids, always out straight, Emma chasing after Angus who she loved most of all.
    I never did get it clean after the men drug her dead from the manure pit. Months 'fore Angus could tell of finding her boots, arranged so neat. A sock over the top of each one to keep it from the muck. Angus always thought that pit too close to the barn. Gonna put a fence around it. Afraid for his cows.
    That pit sucked Emma down like quicksand and never gave her back. Sometimes I wonder if it got Angus too.
    Strange, the little things that break your heart. Like sweet-grass, strewn across the winter floor.
    Catherine-Billy was 15 when we lost Emma-Lucille. Catherine-Billy's most all heart. And what Emma's dying didn't break Lucy's did.
    Catherine-Billy still swears she never gonna have no babies. And she might just be right 'cos she's so riled up over women's rights, I suspect she's scaring the men off.
    Folks in Benign Harbour think duties are all the rights women can handle so she had few friends here sides me. She's teaching up at the college now, so things are better for her.
    It just come to me sudden like Gladie, the day she came home from high school early. She slam-banged her way to the kitchen. I was trying to have a cup of tea. She's waving a piece a paper in the air and looking ready to explode. I grabbed the paper and read it out loud:
    THE 1881 STATUTES OF THIS COUNTRY CANADA DEFINE DISABLED PERSONS AS ANY INFANT, LUNATIC, IDIOT OR MARRIED WOMAN.
    I said, "Brilliant."
    "Mom."
    "Ah, Catherine-Billy think about it. They're telling what we already know—a woman doesn't have a disability till she marries

one."

We got more than one fine example of that right here in Benign Harbour.

Take Silas Simms. Take Silas Simms. Pretty sure that's what his wife Audrey prayed every day of their life together. Dear God, please take Silas.

What a bastard he was and how much better off his family is without him. He drank the food out of their mouths, gambled away their firewood and beat them all, wife, kids. Threw his old mother down the stairs one time. There's some say he even worried his sheep!

Alive he was trouble for everyone. Dead he was still trouble for me.

My Ma always said, "Ida-Mae sticks out like a duck egg in a robin's nest." Only place I managed to fit here in Benign Harbour was the wake house. Angus calls me the darlin' of the funeral parlour.

Folks say I got a gift for huntin' out what people did best and speaking up at every wake, tellin' it good and true. Not always easy finding what some folks did best—not so you can talk about it in church, any rate.

The harder the hunt, the more visitors cram the wake house. It's not respect for dead or living. They're waitin' on me, waitin' to see me stuck for words or caught up in a lie.

I usually go to the wake on the first day so as not to hold people up, but like I said, Silas Simms was given me trouble. And Bernice Bates wasn't helpin'. She called three times. Bernice's the head of the Bingo for Jesus group and they were right worried that Silas wouldn't a gone over by Saturday night, the wake house and the bingo hall being one and the same. We were well into the third day when Angus says, "Come on Ida-Mae. Can't keep Silas from the devil forever." That got me movin'.

It's August and hot. Everybody jammed tight and sweaty into that windowless basement. And no flowers to cover up.

Oh Gladie, there's a lie! There is one floral tribute, from Silas's mom. Angus thinks she's so old she don't remember what a bastard she gave birth to, but I think she knows what she is doing. It's a wrong-side-up horseshoe of red roses with GOOD LUCK SON in gold foil. I think she's laughing the whole time Silas's luck is pouring out.

Hardest of all for me is Audrey. She's the widow and my good friend. She can't imagine how I'm gonna find any damn little thing Silas did that didn't hurt someone, let alone something he was best at.

Truth was I can't imagine it either.

I can't seem to get myself straight and I fidget all the way to the hall, pullin' rough on my dress one minute, my hat the next. I can't breathe. My girdle's too tight and I can hear them "hush-shushing, here she is" by the time I reach the door.

Steppin' through I feel like Moses partin' the Red Sea.

Goes so quiet, you can hear a tick swallow.

Audrey's standin' by the horseshoe. Someone's righted it so what luck Silas has left will stay put but now the letters is upside-down. Audrey's wound so tight, her ears is restin on her shoulders. I take her hands in mine and I say, "Audrey dear," and I don't bother to whisper. "Audrey dear, there's no one could smoke a cigarette as fast as himself."

So ya see I even found somethin' to say for the likes of Silas Simms. I had no words for me father. Him, I buried.

I gotta get. Can't let Maud-Bernice catch me out here. She's driving home tonight. Worried about me here alone. If she finds me in the barn talkin' to the cow, she'll think I'm missing Angus. Love love love, she'll be on at it the whole visit. Always wantin' to know What about love? and I say What about love?

Grade 7, she was already telling me, "I'm in love, Ma. I just think about George and me face gets hot. I can't catch my breath. I'm dizzy, me hands sweat. I get goose bumps."

"Girl, the things you're feelin' are the self-same things small animals feel when they're about to be eaten."

Maud-Bernice'll tell me I must be lonely. I'm not so sure. No doubt about it, Angus fallin' off the barn roof is an ending. There's no way we can be here like we was. But am I lonely? Maud-Bernice is all lonely herself these days.

You see Gladie, after fourteen years on their couch, her Arnold stood up, right in the middle of Oprah, adjusted his privates, put his ball-hat on sideways, and walked out. For good.

Maud started crying in the pickles so I laid a hand on her arm and said, "Wait a bit, girl, you'll see. No man in your life is a damn sight better than no life in your man."

I gotta get to bed. Who am I trying to fool? These days once I'm awake, I'm awake.

Was a time when most of the kids were teenagers, I could answer the phone any hour of the night, deal with whoever, roll over and be back asleep just like that.

Of all the kids, John-Angus got the most calls about himself. He was my first boy child and he'd fought being born, fought it gum and nail. I swear he kept his knees hooked over my bowels and an ovary in each tight fist. I fought too, yelling and carrying on.

"It's a Boy!" they said and all I could hold in my mind was, What in the name of God am I gonna do with a boy?

Best advice I got on having a boy was what my Ma wrote me: It's real good to remember to fold his paraphernalia over before you fasten his diaper.

Girls were crazy for John-Angus. Seemed I was on the phone, day and night, cleaning up his messes.

The last call I got for him—just before he moved out west—the sun was coming up. It was Doc Clayton on the phone. Seems he'd had to do some surgery and could we pick John-Angus up 'cos his truck was still parked down the wharf road. Seemed John-Angus and his date, Sylvie Bates—that would be Bernice's middle girl—had hit a snag. His foreskin was cruelly skewered on her almost perfect barbed wire teeth.

Bernice grabbed the phone from Doc Clayton to take me to task over 'the touch and go upbringing of that cocky bastard John-Angus'.

I wasn't having none of it. I said, "Bernice Bates, you be thankful your girl was with a boy had sense enough to save his own skin." She gasps and I keep right on, "Bernice Bates, you know it had to be John-Angus callin' out for help. We wouldn't expect a child of yours to talk with her mouth full, now would we?"

(Laughs.)

Oh! Thought I heard Maud-Bernice's car. The way the lane wanders, you can't see someone coming till they're here, unless you're perched up top of the hill out back of the barn.

Spent a lot of time on that hill when the kids were small. I particularly remember one day we walked up over the hill to the old MacPherson place. Hippies in it then. Magnificent view of the graveyard. I sat down to nurse baby Bert. The boys were chasin' one another but the four girls kept close by. Maud-Bernice was nigh on to being a woman so I thought it time to start the girl thinking about the other side of love so I told her right out: "There's two kinds of men, those who want sex and"—I pointed to the graveyard—"those who don't."

As soon as I said it I knew them weren't the right words. I was just fed up, wanting to rush the kids, grow them up. Right then I wanted to be done with it all. The farm. The work. But mostly Angus.

Seemed to me I was forever thinkin' I was leavin' Angus. One summer I wore out 2 brand-spankin' pair of shoes walkin' away. Never made it past the end of the lane. Six thousand, six hundred and thirty-six steps from the front door to the main road.

SOUND: cow mooing

IDA-MAE
How do I know that?

Well, I'll tell ya, Gladie. Me and Angus was over to Pictou, visitin' his sister for the day. Just had the two girls and I was heavy with the third. It was a treat to have someone catering to us all and we were late for home. A blizzard caught us halfway and there was no driving up the lane. The drift at the end was that deep and wide. I couldn't seem to stop thinkin' how tired I was and how cold the house would be, like as not the kindling wet. And the barn not done. The girls pulled from the car started bawlin' and that was it for me. "I'm not for here Angus MacHine," I said real loud, yellin' against the wind. And quick as sin he hands me the keys, scoops up Maud and Avis and heads up the lane.

There I was alone with a choice that was no choice at all. I put one foot in front of the other six thousand, six hundred and thirty-six times, following my life up that lane.

I once told Lucy I needed to take every one of them steps to get away from Angus. And Lucy said, "No, ya just need to take the first step six thousand, six hundred and thirty-six times. And, Ida-Mae, you're not ready!"

She was right. Always somethin' stopped me. Pulled me back. Someone whose livin' needed my attention. It'd always be like that. Or so I thought. Now what is there?

SOUND: cow mooing

IDA-MAE
Ah, an old cow. An old woman.

In all me and Angus' time together I never once considered himself leavin' me. But no doubt about it—I am the one left. Never mind it wasn't what he had in his head, climbin' up on that roof. If ya ask me, nothing in his head at all. Up there tryin' to fix what could easy wait. Or worse tryin' to fix what can't ever be.

Course I'm bad as Angus tryin' to fix what's past. I keep diggin' me father up—buryin' him again and again. Deeper and deeper when maybe buryin' is not the thing I should be doin'.

I kept trying to convince myself that leavin' Angus would fix all me problems. It was the only way I could believe I'd really go—soon as I was done nursin', soon as the kids were old enough. As soon as Angus got over losing Emma. Soon as Lucy's gone. As soon as, as soon as.

I was comin' in from this barn the night, it hit me I'd not ever be ready. The house was lit up and it seemed I could see all the way inside to where Angus was tryin' his best to learn chess from Bert.

It struck me just then that Emma's dyin' gave Angus his children more surely than I did.

And I fancied I could see the girls upstairs with Maud-Bernice's new record player...And Lucy, elbows into a sink full a dishes, her head turned round answerin' a question—geography or how do ya spell Mississippi, and her doin' that funny little thing she always did ippississim. Ippississim

I heard one of the boys laugh—John Angus, I think.

And there I was outside—caught—halfway home, halfway gone and not one livin' soul needin' me. And me knowin' I was never gonna leave Angus MacHine.

But all that was a long way from my knowin' that day up on the hill. All I knew was how bad I needed to be anywhere but here.

When we got home, I put on a clean dress. The only decent one I had to wear while I was nursing and Lord knows I was always nursing. Or so it seemed on days like this.

SOUND: cow mooing

IDA-MAE
Ah, Gladie, it wasn't the babies so much as that damn dress. It buttoned up the front. Easy access. I was tired of that. Seemed to me my whole damn life someone'd been tryin' to get somethirg off me, squeezin' past the last drop of whatever I had worth havin'.

I was dry, 'cept for forty bucks I'd kept aside. I was planning on a new dress. One I could hardly get into myself.

I got to town walkin' and on the whole God-forsakin' street there's no one save me and some old woman, with a dress fit worse than mine and two left boots, one flat, other well-heeled. We walk to meet. Gunslingers. I'm thinking, yeah / I got money / me / Ida-Mae / I saved it / and no one / not Angus / not kids / and for sure not some damn charity case, is gonna get it. She limps past, shoots me with dead-dog eyes.

Shakes me up, that look. I go for a coffee, check the diaper pin in my bra, pat the money.

Ermaline, who works the counter, was all of a twitter, "Pathetic old woman, that. Been around about a week. No one knows where she's sleeping and no one's seen her eat. They say her whole family got burnt up while she was off somewhere, drinking. They say she carries what's left of their bones around in a paper bag. The old fool lost it day before yesterday."

    I go back outside. Shove the forty bucks right at her, hating her for being sensical enough to take it. That money disappeared quicker than a snake into a stone wall. She grabs my arm and we start walking, slow, searching, poking garbage, shaking hedges. We cried together one time when we found the wrong bag. I know it sounds desperate sad but I was starting to feel real good.

    Dark came and we kept on right past Ermaline gawking out the shop door, down the road, across the fields, up the long lane, past Angus, gawking out the barn door and right up to the house. I'm anxious to get in. She stops me on the top step and says, "Name's Lucy," and slips that wad of twos into the pocket of my dress.

    I say, "We're home Lucy," though I never am sure which one of us needed the tellin'.

    This here's Lucy's hat. Wear it a lot.

    She was the only livin' soul I ever told what my father done to me.

    I told her how his weight—forcin' the air from my lungs—was greater that what one man's weight should ever be. Bearin' down on me. His whole body rank with what I'd not ever mistake for love again.

    I said how I had no breasts so he didn't bother with the unbuttoning. For weeks I wore a crooked line of black to purple to yellow buttons down my front. And the almost woman I was, wanted to undo them buttons and peel off that dirty skin.

    I told how it was as quiet in that barn. "Like it is right now, Lucy," I said.

    As it is right now.

    And I spoke of years later helpin' one of the kids with their homework and there it was right in the book—how the body is always shedding skin. I tried to figger how long it'd take to get a whole new skin one flake at a time. How long til it wasn't me in this barn at all.

Lucy wasn't one to give an answer where there was none. She was most a listener.

She and Angus hardly spoke at all, even though she was with us for years. "How are ya now?" is about the most he ever said to Lucy and she'd smile and nod and say nothing.

She'd been here three years the one time she answered him. She was in the rocker in the kitchen and Angus was just after bringing me and the new baby home.

"How are ya now?"

And she answered him, "Dying."

He handed her the baby and said, "This here's Emma-Lucille. The Lucille part's for you."

She gave him a look, the mischief flashing in her eyes, and said, "How are ya now, Angus MacHine?"

Oh Lordy, I forgot Angus and his queer dream. That's what got me out here in the first place.

Himself is not the only one to be havin' queer dreams. For years after Angus left off growin' zucchini I was still dreamin' of sex with Red Hughie. Angus'd be there, too—standin' at the foot of the bed, mumblin' about strange men plantin' God only knows what in his garden.

Red'd just be getting' to the meat & potatoes, buttonin' down his pants and there IT would be—an overripe zucchini and I'd wake every time wonderin' if me and Angus had put by enough to see us through.

Years now since I woke feeling empty from a dream. Least ways it was until the night after Angus fell off the barn.

That night I dreamed me and Angus were hanging on to opposite ends of an old rope that was laying over the peak. We couldn't see, nor hear each other. The strands were letting go. Kids gone, one strand, livestock sold off. Another strand. I'd no sooner thought about Emma-Lucille when a whole bunch let go at once.

Ya know, Gladie, you're all that's here living 'cept me and God-willing Angus. Your goin' will be another strand.

Me and Angus should be goin', too. Before the rope gives way. Or

one of us lets go.
 Ya know, Gladie, talking to you's like talking to Angus. You don't say much and I'm never sure how much ya understand.
 Good night, Gladie.

> *SOUND: cow mooing*

IDA-MAE
Some nights Angus'd come in from this barn so horny even his feet were swollen. I'd follow the manured boots that tracked his intentions through the house. Nights like those I disposed of Angus quickly. Butter should churn so fast.
Actually, I preferred butter. Softer, less clingy and you almost always had something to show for your time.
Ah, come home Angus.

> *SOUND: cow mooing*

IDA-MAE
The cow misses you.

> *She crosses to the wall, hits the light switch.*
> *LIGHTS OUT. CLOSING MUSIC up for the end of the show, then out as the LIGHTS UP for the curtain call.*

From page to stage: "Her Father's Barn"

"Her Father's Barn" began during a long car ride. I was thinking about a lady (mother of 21) who lived near me and these words took on a life of their own. Ida-Mae was born and bred, and bred and bred...in the country.
So began *The Ida-Mae Poems*. They were published in several literary journals and appear in my poetry collection *The Dead can't Dance*.
Pauline Liengme, who unbeknownst to me was a passionate and well loved actor, approached me to ask if I had considered turning those poems into a monologue. I looked at her as if she was crazy. Years later she told me that my look had frightened her more than approaching me had.
I was skeptical. Not only were the poems written from a third person perspective but Ida-Mae and I were different women from different worlds. We didn't think or speak like one another. I suspect we didn't even breathe the same. The first half took me three years, the second three months.
Pauline became my Ida-Mae and garnered awards in Nova Scotia, Ontario and British Columbia.

-PCM

"Her Father's Barn" production history:

Atlantic Fringe Festival (NS) 2001
Festival Antigonish Late Night (NS) 2002
London Fringe [ON] 2005
Liverpool International Play Festival (NS) 2006
Uno Festival [BC] 2007
Mulgrave Theatre [NS] 2008
King's Theatre [NS] 2010

Ida-Mae—from poem to play

Pauline Liengme

It was just going be the usual annual one-act play festival, or so I thought. Little did I know that this one was to change my life in so many ways.

The programme was a bit short so a local poet, Pam Calabrese (don't forget the broccoli} Maclean, was asked to do a reading, and she chose her Ida-Mae poems. I was enthralled. In these short poems I was seeing a gritty, humorous, downtrodden, yet victorious woman leaping off the page. Writing like this was extraordinary but yelled out for more and more.

I went home and could not get her out of my mind—both the character and the author. Therein was a problem—the author! She scared me rotten and even though I knew I had to talk to her I also knew I would need a lot of courage to do it!

So there I am in the foyer of the Bauer Theatre and there she was, surrounded by a load of fans and well wishers (this women had a LOT of fans in Antigonish and quite a few of them were the town eccentrics). I thought myself into a Lady Bracknell pose and said, "Excuse me."

The entourage moved aside and, as she wrote in the eventual play, "it was like the partin' of the Red Sea."

"Your Ida-Mae poems should be a play which you must write."

"Really?" was the reply.

"Yes, and I would like to play her."

Now, where did that come from? At that moment I realized that Ida-Mae was already in my head and growing. However, the entourage flowed back, and the conversation was over, and I thought that was the end of it.

A couple of years (yes, I do mean years) later, this MacLean woman tapped me on the shoulder and said, "Here it is" and gave me the first draft of Her Father's Barn. Boy, was I scared or what?

She had done it and now I had to do my part.

We started to meet and go over the script, me adding my stagecraft input and Pam (for by now we were on first name terms) keeping the poetry of the language all the time.

Then the growth began, both to the play and to the character inside me.

It is very hard to describe how good writing can seep into your heart and, without any trouble at all, you 'know' your character. You can see her in other situations away from the play itself. I know what Ida-Mae has for breakfast—if Angus would give her the time to have any. I know how she manages her poverty, her passionate and intense sexuality, how she loves her children and, for the brief time it took to conceive them all, how she loved the eight men who were necessary. Angus she loves all the time, although, as with all great loves, there were times she didn't think so.

As Ida-Mae, the play, author and actor grew, so did our relationship. Each moment together gave indescribable happiness and comfort. We have always been there for each other through many ups and downs and LOTS of hilarious laughter! The stories we could tell—like at the Liverpool International Play Festival where not only did I try and order at a Tim Horton's by speaking to the garbage can, but we suddenly found the nightdress for Ida-Mae was covered in mouse droppings (it had been stored in our old barn). After washing it in the dressing room sink, I went on stage in a wet nightie!

How at the Khyber where we played in a windowless room but, because it was a matinee, Pam thought she wouldn't need a flashlight behind the 'barn wall' to see her mooing cues! (You should know that the stage lighting is limited to one bare bulb for the play.)

I could go on telling you about the heartbreak and the deep, deep agony that Ida-Mae endures that, all the time, rides along with the laughter and secret wickedness in which she delights. All of this comes from my heart too but I couldn't have it any other way.

We have received many accolades for HFB but they are worth nothing compared with the love and friendship that a poetic farm woman and an uptight come-from-away have found and enjoy together. What a pair we are!!

Pauline played Ida-Mae in the play's premiere.

Pam Calabrese MacLean

Janitor

Time
Now.

Setting
A nursing home bedroom. There is a good-size table beside the bed that holds a telephone and several stand-up photos of a young boy up to age 10. There is also a glass of water with a bendy straw in it. There is a large a stand-up, customized calendar on the table —Tuesday, July15th. The calendar is one day per page so Florence can see it from the bed. It is a 'catastrophes throughout history' calendar, and the story for each day is printed below the day and date.

There is a chair near the foot of the bed. There is a garbage can beside the table.

Centre stage in the hallway opposite Florence's room there is a large potted plant.

Scene change:
The change from one day to the next involves dimming the lights, Ulysses taking a page off Florence's calendar, tossing it into Florence's trash can. He then mops his way out of the room, around the plant, and lights come up when he re-enters.

Pam Calabrese MacLean

Cast

Florence, an elderly resident
Ulysses, a janitor in his twenties. He is wearing a baseball hat and hospital scrubs. He speaks with an extreme stutter, which we indicate the first time he speaks. It is up to the actor to do the rest.

Janitor

Day 1 Tuesday July 15th

FLORENCE lies stiffly in bed. Her hands lie unmoving on top of the covers. ULYSSES is mopping the floor downstage.

FLORENCE
(Calling feebly)
Edmund. Edmund.

Ulysses looks all around.

FLORENCE
(Calls louder)
Edmund. Edmund.
(Louder still)
Edmund! Edmund! Answer your Mother.

Ulysses ducks as if to avoid being hit.

FLORENCE
Who's there? Where is Edmund?
 What are you doing? Come here so I can get a look.

Ulysses does not move.

FLORENCE
Did you hear me? Come *here*!

Ulysses moves forward but not too close.

FLORENCE
Who in blazes are you? Not the regular guy. Make yourself useful and rip the day off, yeah?

> *Ulysses looks at her questioningly and moves a little closer to the table.*

FLORENCE
Rip the day off the calendar. I like to get a jump on tomorrow!
   Why is it so damned cold in here?
   You dumb? Or just stupid?
   Speak up or I'll wash your dirty mouth out with that mop. The mop, the mop, look out, the mop?

> *Ulysses smiles.*

FLORENCE
Your mama read that book to you too? Edmund loved it!
   Give me a drink like a good boy.

> *Ulysses makes a disgusted face.*

FLORENCE
Not so fond of the 'good boy'?
   Come on! Just a little drink.
   Would it be at my bedside if it was going to kill me?
   And would it be so bad if it did? Certainly wouldn't matter to you!

> *Ulysses is uncomfortable but holds out the glass to her. Florence does not move to take it.*

FLORENCE
You're going to have to put the straw in my mouth. A hot drink

would be better.

> *Florence speaks slowly, separating her words as if speaking to an idiot.*

FLORENCE
I   can't   move   my   hands.

> *Ulysses approaches holding the bendy straw for Florence. Florence growls and snaps at his hand like a mad dog. Ulysses puts down the glass and mops up the spilled water. Then he moves to leave.*

FLORENCE
Rip the day off on your way.
(laughs cruelly)

> *Blackout.*

Day 2 Wednesday July 16

> *Ulysses is mopping. Everything is much the same as the day before. Florence appears to be sleeping. Ulysses is being very quiet. He keeps looking nervously over at the bed.*
> *The mop clangs against the bed and Ulysses stops, waits three beats and resumes mopping.*
> *He hits the bed a second time.*

FLORENCE
Edmund? Edmund.

> *Ulysses groans.*

FLORENCE

Oh, it's you. Don't you ever get a day off? My ears are still ringing from yesterday's chatter!
   No sense of humour either.
   Hurry up and get out of here, I'm expecting someone.
   Edmund. He telephoned. Got stranded in a blizzard.

   Both look at the calendar on the table.

FLORENCE
It's winter somewhere!
   Death watch lady tells me your name is Ulysses.
   Well at least your mother has sense of humour.
   Got a girlfriend?
   Live with her?
   What? No lead in your pencil?

   Beat.

FLORENCE
You don't still live with mommy, Uly?
(pronounced like Julie)
   Boys don't love their mothers enough.
   You love your mother, Uly?
   It's your job to love her.
   I'm betting you don't do a great job?
   It's the same with all you boys.

   Ulysses' head snaps up.

FLORENCE
You are alive! Surely someone loves you enough to call you Uly!
   No?
   Whatever?
   What did you do to your mother, Uly?
   I'm being a good Mom and hanging on until Edmund gets here.
   He's my son. He doesn't love me.

You work here long? I've been here forever!
Kind of lonely. Probably why I so look forward to our scintillating banter!
Talk to me, Uly.
You know what. Forget it. I'm tired.
I've had migraines that were more fun than you!

> *Ulysses moves toward the exit.*

FLORENCE
(Almost a whisper)
Uly!

> *Ulysses turns back.*
> *Florence gives him the finger.*
> *Ulysses stares at her hand.*
> *Florence wiggles all 10 fingers at the calendar.*

FLORENCE
It's a miracle Uly. A frickin' miracle.

> *Ulysses gives her the finger.*
> *Lights dim.*

Day 3 Thursday July 17

> *Lights up as Ulysses enters.*
> *Florence is asleep. Ulysses decides he can use her phone. He picks up the receiver. Clicks the button a few times.*

FLORENCE
Phone's dead.

> *Ulysses gasps.*

FLORENCE
You thought I was dead too?
    Disappointed?
    You one of those fancy boys?
    Is that what you did to your mother?
    Did I tell you he called?
    Would it be too much to ask you to nod your stupid head for Christ's sake?

    Ulysses looks at the phone.

FLORENCE
Phone was fine yesterday. You probably bumped it with your mop. You bumped everything else!
    Listen Uly, we could work out some gestures…

    Ulysses looks at her hands.

FLORENCE
And yes my fingers worked yesterday. Can't get anything past you! You could gesture and I'd get some answers!

    Ulysses mops toward the exit.

FLORENCE
You missed a spot!
    What's for supper? I could do with a hot meal. Gloop is one thing but congealed—great word.
    Any chance you know where to get a blanket?
    Listen, son—

    Ulysses reacts angrily.

FLORENCE
You don't like 'son' any more than 'be a good boy! Whatever you did to your mother, it must have been something pretty bad.

Kids are rotten little bastards and everything they do, they do *to* their mothers. Why do you think Edmund's still not here?
You're not getting this, are you?
It's cold in here.

Florence thumps her heart.

FLORENCE
And in here.

Lights dim.

Day 4 Friday July 18

Ulysses, with no mop or bucket, enters carrying two take-out cups. He puts them on the table and takes a checker board from under his arm and the checkers in a baggy from his pocket. Florence is propped up and looks a little perkier.

FLORENCE
What are you doing in here if not working? Planning to steal a little something?
What you got there?

ULYSSES
Hhhhot.

FLORENCE
'Hot'...? Oh, I love charades! Second word...

ULYSSES
(Blurts)
Chocolate!

FLORENCE
Alleluia! Another fricken' miracle. This room is a regular Saint Anne de Bo Peep! Right, Uly?

ULYSSES
(struggles to speak)
Ulysses.

FLORENCE
Kind of pretentious for a janitor.

> *Ulysses sits in the chair and flattens out the checker board on the bed. Florence takes the checkers out of the bag and puts them on the board.*

FLORENCE
I'm all of a sudden too tired. Can we try again tomorrow? You are coming tomorrow? I checked my book and I'm free.

ULYSSES
Not tomorrow.

FLORENCE
Why ever not?

ULYSSES
Vacation.

FLORENCE
When are you back?

ULYSSES
August 5th.

FLORENCE
Be a good boy and give me the calendar.

> *Ulysses hands her the calendar.*
> *Florence throws the checker board and the checkers one by one at Ulysses to drive him backwards out the door. When he is gone, Florence tears pages off the calendar up to August 5th. She lets the pages fall to the floor.*
>   *Florence discovers a red checker (colour Uly used) and as the lights dim she sobs as she puts it under her pillow.*
>   *Lights down.*

Day 5 Saturday July 19

> *Lights up as Ulysses enters with no mop or bucket. He is carrying a shopping bag. He sets it down. Ulysses picks up the checkers and board. He sets them on the chair. He then picks up the pages of the calendar, and yesterday's cups and throws them in the garbage and puts the calendar on the table.*
>   *Florence is asleep, her hair partially obscuring her face. He reaches to touch Florence several times before he manages the courage to brush the hair from her face. Florence does not move.*
>   *Ulysses takes a very brightly-patterned blanket out of the shopping bag and tucks Florence in.*
>   *Lights down.*

Day 6 Friday August 1

> *Lights up. Ulysses enters mopping as before. Mops his way to the calendar and scribbles out the 5 and pens in the 1st. Florence appears to be asleep but is watching Ulysses. Uly knows she's watching.*

FLORENCE
Edmund was here. He brought a blanket. Such a good son! You could learn a thing or two!

ULYSSES
Stop it, Florence! Stop pretending!

FLORENCE
Why would I want to do that?

ULYSSES
It's not helping. You're making yourself sad.

FLORENCE
That's not why I'm sad.

ULYSSES
Sadder, then.
    He isn't here. Why? A blizzard, a broken car, a different excuse every day.
    He can't be here. Isn't that better than him bringing you a blanket and leaving you again?

FLORENCE
Pretty sure of yourself, aren't you?

ULYSSES
And you're lying to yourself!

FLORENCE
Want to know something? Of course you do. More lies are believed than truths. They're easier.
    What are you doing here, anyway? Weren't you going away?

ULYSSES
I came back early. I thought I could help.

FLORENCE
You can't even help yourself.

ULYSSES
I brought you the blanket!

FLORENCE
Good deeds die in the telling.

ULYSSES
I need someone to know.

FLORENCE
And I need to pretend.

ULYSSES
Are you pretending I'm Edmund, right now?

FLORENCE
I will if you will!
   You think I don't know that Edmund has been dead a long, long time.
   I could never be one of those women who lose a child and keep their room as if they'll be back any moment. Praying the dust won't settle.
   His loss has defined my whole life. I let Edmund grow. Saw him a year older every birthday. Listened to him differently. Constructed his life out of nothing. And now he lives in a far city with a wife and I have two grandchildren.
   Do you understand, Uly? I am not alone.

ULYSSES
Being alone is not so bad.

FLORENCE
Until you're dying. And I can't pretend my way out of that one.
　　Edmund's dying was a mistake. A moment of inattention. A little part of the plan forgotten. Not what God intended at all.

ULYSSES
God wasn't paying attention?

FLORENCE
I wasn't paying attention.
　　Enough about me. If, like you say, being alone is not that bad, why are you here?

ULYSSES
How weren't you paying attention, Florence?

FLORENCE
I'm an ugly, mean-spirited woman. I did that to myself. I worked a couple of jobs. Not because I needed to, not really. Married money. Edmund spent more time with other people.
　　I knew I wasn't a good mom, but I was older when I married. Two years in, my philosophy was, "Life's a shit sandwich, every day but a bite. The more bread you have, the less shit you taste!"
　　I wasn't even home when the police came to tell me.

ULYSSES
You were the rotten bastard, not Edmund!

FLORENCE
Ask him when he gets here.

ULYSSES
Jesus, Florence, he's not coming.

FLORENCE
Oh, he's coming, Uly. You just don't know it yet.

ULYSSES: He's dead. Pretending he's still alive—

FLORENCE
Not as pathetic as it sounds.

ULYSSES
If you say so.

FLORENCE
The best thing about it? Sometimes I forget I'm pretending.

> *Lights dim as Ulysses exits.*

Day 7 Friday August 1

> *There is a soft light burning beside Florence's bed. She is under a mound of blankets. Ulysses' blanket is on top. Ulysses is close to the bed, peering at her face through the dark.*

FLORENCE:
Not dead.

ULYSSES
Not sleeping, either.

FLORENCE
I meant you. Not dead. You stayed away a long time.

ULYSSES
I told you I was going. And I came back early.

FLORENCE
Didn't want to miss me on my way out, eh?

ULYSSES
Something like that, yah.

FLORENCE
I'm glad you came back. I've been waiting. But why did you come back?

ULYSSES
I need to be forgiven.

FLORENCE
I'm not your mother.

ULYSSES
I know.

FLORENCE
How can I—?

ULYSSES
You need forgiveness, too.

FLORENCE
Now how in the name of the nine blind, snotty orphans can we do that?

ULYSSES
I'm not sure. Trust would be a good start.
   You're shivering.

FLORENCE
It's getting late for new starts for me.

ULYSSES
Maybe forgiveness comes in the asking.

FLORENCE
Seems awful easy. Am I your penance? Are you mine?

> *Ulysses moves behind the bed and rubs the blankets covering Florence's back and shoulders. Florence continues to shiver.*

ULYSSES
You said that we all have things we can't bear to look at. I can't look at myself.
   I make my definition of love out of things I don't have and if I get lucky enough to cross something off, I add two. A list with no end in sight.
   I thought it was you afraid to let someone love you. I thought my Mother was afraid to let me love her. I'm the one who's afraid. It's too late to tell her.
   I can't go back I can't go forward. I'm stuck.
   I don't know what to do.

> *Ulysses climbs in behind Florence. He wraps his arms around her. He snuggles in as close as he can.*
>   *Florence sobs.*

ULYSSES
Hush. Hush. I'm here.

FLORENCE
Edmund? Edmund.

ULYSSES
I'm here.

FLORENCE
Edmund.

ULYSSES
Hush.

FLORENCE
Ulysses.

ULYSSES
Uly.

Lights down.

The end.

The Seeds for "Janitor"

I originally called "Janitor" "Forgiveness". But can you ask forgiveness of someone other than the person you wronged? That question threw a different, clearer insight into Florence and Ulie's journeys.

The day my Dad had his accident we argued before I caught the school bus. He made me kiss his cheek—a grudging truce. He went to work. I never saw him again even though he lived nine days. He didn't want me to see what the fire had done. Wanted me to remember him other than scorched. I was so angry that he would keep me away, I remember whispering, *maybe he'll die.*

That guilt would have been with me forever were it not for a hospital roommate, years later. She was elderly and her suitcase of guilt was as heavy as mine. Neither one of us knew what we should do to help each other. We talked late into the night and were so painfully honest that by the time of my discharge we were both less burdened.

Whether our destinations were the same or different, we learned that we could travel together. In the end our directions like Florence and Ulie's were different, but our destination was a shared one. Permission. Permission to forgive ourselves.

-PCM

Pam Calabrese MacLean

Is it Wednesday?

Time
Now.

Setting
A bench, possibly at a bus stop.

Cast

Mavis, an elderly woman
Stella, an elderly woman

Pam Calabrese MacLean

Is it Wednesday?

>*MAVIS and STELLA are sitting on a bench.*

MAVIS
Waiting for the bus?

STELLA
Is it Wednesday?

MAVIS
I'll check my pill case.

STELLA
I used to check my underwear!

MAVIS
I still do!

STELLA
I mean those days of the week panties.

MAVIS
Saturday wore out way before the others.

>*Stella looks confused.*

MAVIS
Traffic!

Stella looks up and down the street, then back at Mavis.

STELLA
How are you?

MAVIS
How are you?

STELLA
Fine. I asked first.

MAVIS
Yes. fine. The kids?

STELLA
I don't have kids.
 Who are you?

MAVIS
I don't think you know me.

STELLA
I'm pretty sure I do.

MAVIS
I don't think I have children. either.

STELLA
I have two—one of each.

MAVIS
Each what?

STELLA
Each and other go together well.

Sofa

MAVIS
I like words, too.

STELLA
Do you play Scrabble?

MAVIS
I'm not very good at small talk anymore.

STELLA
I'm not very good at anything anymore.

MAVIS
Do you remember your first time?

STELLA
The first time I wasn't good at something?

MAVIS
No! THE FIRST TIME!

STELLA
On the bus?

MAVIS
Your first time was on the bus!

STELLA
Oh, *that* first time.

MAVIS
I remember my last.

STELLA
Me too. Long term memory is still good.
    I called it the F-depression: fat, fifty, uckless and frustrated.

63

Long beat.

MAVIS
Uckless doesn't start with 'F'. It might not even be a word.
   Never mind. What was it like?

STELLA
Do you make dill pickles?

MAVIS
Are we still talking about what we were talking about?

STELLA
Entertainment.

MAVIS
Do you go to the entertainments here? There's a special one next week.

STELLA
You wrap up something you don't want anymore and give it to someone else.

MAVIS
Re-gifting, it's called.

STELLA
There's a name for it? What a horrible word.

MAVIS
A verb, no less!

STELLA
If they start making verbs out of nouns, there'll be a lot more I can't do!

MAVIS
Well, I can still hat myself. And unhat myself and if I go out twice in one day. I can re-hat myself and—

STELLA
The mad hatter!
   I have lots of lovely scarves. I'll gift one of those. Then someone can scarf themselves.

MAVIS
Isadora Duncan.

   Stella looks confused.

MAVIS
She scarfed herself!
   Wonder do they take husbands?

STELLA
Hard to wrap.

MAVIS
Duct tape.

STELLA
What were we talking about?

MAVIS
Sex.

STELLA
I had sex for the last time 25 years ago. I don't remember much except that Stanley died.

MAVIS
During?

STELLA
Don't they always?

MAVIS
I remember every detail of my last time. Just as if it was this morning.

STELLA
Was it?

MAVIS
What?

STELLA
This morning?

MAVIS
Yes. Do you have a ticket?

STELLA
I didn't know I needed one.

MAVIS
Well they're not going to let you climb on without it!

    Stella does a mouth open gormless look.

MAVIS
The bus.

STELLA
I'm not really going on the bus.

MAVIS
Oh.

STELLA
Not allowed.

MAVIS
Me either. Every bus driver knows it too!

STELLA
I like to walk right over to the bus...I stare at the driver talking on his little radio.

MAVIS
My husband takes me on the bus sometimes.

STELLA
A person has to get to the bank.

MAVIS
You still keep your money in the bank?

STELLA
Where do you keep yours?

MAVIS
My husband tells me there's a scam.

STELLA
That's scary.

MAVIS
It's all to do with money.

STELLA
Our money?

MAVIS
Don't sign anything.

STELLA
I won't.

MAVIS
Won't what?

STELLA
Sign anything.

MAVIS
Why? What did you hear?

STELLA
I don't have any money to worry about. I think I work for the government. They send me cheques, pay my rent.

MAVIS
I worry about money all the time. What will we do when ours is gone?

STELLA
Government will pay.

MAVIS
I don't want charity.
    Besides, why did I scrimp and save my whole life? You're here with no money living the same as me with lots of money. I could have spent it all and been here like you with no money.

STELLA
(Taken aback)
It's the same with liquor. When you have it there are all kinds of people around. And when you don't the government pays.

MAVIS
I like a little drink at bed time. Helps me get to sleep before the

snoring!

STELLA
Tea?

MAVIS
I wish they didn't boil the tea at the entertainments.

STELLA
I'm going to wrap up one of my scarves. I have a lot of lovely scarves.
   What are you taking?

MAVIS
Two pink, a blue and vigaro.

STELLA
Viagra. A re-gift of a re-lift at the entertainments!

MAVIS
I have to miss out. John is taking me shopping.

STELLA
I have a brother named John.

MAVIS
Where is he?

STELLA
I don't know. Do you like games?

MAVIS
We used to play Scrabble a lot. Uckless isn't a word. I checked the dictionary.

STELLA
You didn't go anywhere!

MAVIS
Didn't I?

STELLA
Stanley and I played Probe.

MAVIS
I bet you did!
    I can't remember the last time.

STELLA
Yes you can. This morning.

MAVIS
Who told you that?

STELLA
We used to play with another couple.

MAVIS
I never could imagine the logistics of that. At some point do the men kiss each other? Only seems fair. John wouldn't like that.

STELLA
Probe is a word game. We played Tuesday evenings. Why is it I remember that but haven't found my hearing aid for a week?
    Of course I could have said Thursday. You wouldn't know the difference.

MAVIS
You mean you wouldn't know the difference. It was Thursday.

STELLA
I hope not. That's the entertainments night. I wonder what I'll give away.

MAVIS
You have lots of nice scarves.

STELLA
Do you know what I regret forgetting most? The people I loved. I've lost the people I loved.

MAVIS
Droppin' like F in uckless!.

STELLA
Some are lost in my head. I can't figure out where they've gone.
    Like my brother John. He was married to my very best friend. I've lost track of her too.
    My friend and I met at Business College. Ate lunch on a bench like this one every nice day. Then we got jobs in the same building. She was on the 5th floor and I on the 3rd. We still had lunch together.

MAVIS
Did you meet on the 4th?

STELLA
Of July? No, Christmas. She came home with me and met John. I married Stanley.

MAVIS
I married John.

STELLA
And then we lived our lives. Had our children, first days of school, graduations, weddings, retirements and somehow after Stanley

died we ended up here. I can almost remember us on this bench.

We stood for each other. My dress was very plain. She looked like a princess.

Oh I remember—she shocked everyone. A bride in pale pink. You can just imagine the speculation. "What, almost a virgin?"

How sad is that? Losing your brother and your friend. I sit out here hoping that my friend—

MAVIS
Oh my God, I'm your friend!

STELLA
That's very kind of you—

MAVIS
No it's me. I'm me. You're you. We're we. Us. Friends. The friends. My husband. Your brother. We did the school, the jobs…Scrabble…

STELLA
Oh dear I'm afraid you're mistaken. I don't think I know you.

MAVIS
I'm pretty sure you do.

STELLA
Here's the bus.

MAVIS
Are you meeting someone?

STELLA
Is it Wednesday?

The end.

A bench is a bench is a bench

My Mom called on Friday to invite my friend Pauline and me for a special tea party on Sunday. That was all the information she would share. Mom lived three hours away so it wasn't a quick trip.

Pauline and I headed out early Sunday. We made good time. We regaled one another with dementia stories, neither saying that we thought my Mom was a good way down that hill already.

I told Pauline of my most recent trip: Mom and I were all ready to go shopping. Mom flew into a rage because she couldn't go ANYWHERE with me looking like that! She turned and was out the door heading for the elevator.

By the time I had locked up she was gone. I raced down the seven flights of stairs and was standing in front of the elevator doors (hardly puffing at all) when she stepped out.

She was overjoyed. What a nice surprise! When did I get here? Did I want to go shopping?

This trip, Mom was nowhere to be found. Her apartment was locked so Pauline and I sat on a bench near the elevator. We were tired and more than a little silly. And our minds were on dementia.

Suddenly silent, Pauline and I hold hands, reminded once again of all that can be lost.

Along came 'Is it Wednesday?'

-PCM

Pam Calabrese MacLean

Peppermints

Time
Now.

Setting
Begins and ends in a nursing home.

Cast

Jillia, An older woman
Ray, An older man
Intercom voice

Pam Calabrese MacLean

Peppermints

Scene 1: Nursing home

Lights up on RAY and JILLIA behind a hospital screen. Audience sees silhouette of Jillia sitting on the bed while Ray is removing her clothes. She is hitting at him, resisting.

RAY
No peppermint for you Missy!

She settles, lets him finish and pull her nightgown over her head. He tucks her in and tries to lie down with her.

JILLIA
Get out. Out. My father will hear us.

She begins to scream and Ray quickly gets out of bed and moves to a chair outside the curtain. He takes the bag of peppermints from his pocket.

RAY
I remember the first candy I gave you.

Lights down.

Scene 2: Train station

> *Jillia is sitting on a bench. Ray approaches SR.*

RAY
Could a seat next to a lovely woman such as yourself be acquired with a peppermint?

JILLIA
You're so slick you'll slide right off the bench.

RAY
Guessing you don't know me well enough to want to anchor me. My name is Ray. Raymond R. Reginald Esq.
   I think I could fall in love with you, dear!

JILLIA
Oh for the love of all that's good and holy.

> *Beat.*

JILLIA
I'm Jillia and my last name is my husband's.

RAY
Well, sweet lady, I'm 59 and I have been a widower for more than half of that.

JILLIA
Lot of years to be on the prowl.

RAY
Would a candy make you like me more?

JILLIA
(Laughs, crinkling her nose)
No, but I'll take one anyway.

RAY
What do you do, Jillia? Such a pretty name.

JILLIA
An error on my birth certificate. I'm a librarian.

RAY
That makes a lot of sense.

JILLIA
Excuse me?

RAY
You have gravitas, dear lady.

JILLIA
If we're going to talk you need to know how much I despise pet names. If you want me to feel like a dear lady, call me Jillia. please.

RAY
Fair enough, sweet Jillia.

JILLIA
Close enough, slick Ray!

RAY
Where are you headed?

JILLIA
Maybe right here if they can't clear the tracks. Eventually Selkirk.

Pam Calabrese MacLean

RAY
Impossible my d—my, my! The population is too small. There's no possibility of me never having seen you. I, too, am headed there.

JILLIA
You live in Selkirk?

RAY
No but my daughter does. I visit once a month. Grandchildren, you know.

JILLIA
I don't have children. It's hereditary, you know. If your parents had no offspring, chances are neither will you!

RAY
(short pause before he guffaws)
Are you headed home to your lucky husband?

JILLIA
Not so lucky. He's in the Riverview Health Centre here in Winnipeg. Palliative care. I'm back to him in a few days.

RAY
I'm so sorry, Jillia. I apologize for my cavalier flirting. You are very flirtable, but given—

INTERCOM
All aboard. Northbound for Selkirk, Selkirk.

Ray hands Jillia a peppermint and his card.

RAY
Please write if you need a friend—no strings, heart or other.

Sofa

Lights down

Scene 3: Train station

Three years later. Ray and Jillia are wearing noticeably different winter coats. Ray is sitting and Jillia is standing behind the bench. Ray turns around.

RAY
Jillia!

JILLIA
Oh, my. Hello, Ray. What a wonderful sight you are! How are you? How have you been? Found that new love yet?

RAY
You too are a balm for sore eyes. Have I once again found you on your way from your husband in Winnipeg?

JILLIA
In a way.

RAY
In a way?

JILLIA
I still visit Winnipeg, but my Elijah passed a year and a half ago.

RAY
You didn't mention that in your notes. I was always happy to receive them. Even without your last name or return address!

JILLIA
You were uncomfortably tempting!

RAY
I was?

JILLIA
Still are.

RAY
Not too uncomfortable I hope.

Jilllia does her crinkle nose laugh.

RAY
So you still go to Winnipeg. Is Elijah buried there?

JILLIA
No Elijah is buried at home in Selkirk. We never lived anywhere else. I go back to visit. Well, I mean the hospital. Not his actual room. Another family's pain in there.

She turns away, then turns back to him.

JILLIA
Enough about me.

RAY
Is this where you say: Enough about me. Let's talk about you. What do you think of me?

JILLIA
(laughing)
You make me laugh!

RAY
Did Elijah make you laugh?

JILLIA
Yes. And he kept me going. I wish I could've done the same for him. He slipped away while I wasn't paying attention. At least that's how it felt, feels.

RAY
It was the same with Brit. She fell at home. In a coma for days. Brain aneurysm. So quick and no pain.
   I counted her breaths. Talked to her nonstop. I hoped it made her feel settled—I knew she wasn't coming back. I talked so I could remember everything. I nodded off and she let go.

> *Ray pulls a hanky from his pocket and rubs his nose roughly as if to regain control.*

RAY
It still hurts.
   Tell me more about your Elijah.

JILLIA
Only if you have another handkerchief!

> *Ray takes a clean, folded hanky from his pocket and hands it to Jillia.*

JILLIA
Smells like peppermints, Raymond!
   Each time I visited I would stand for a minute outside the hospital, look up at his window. To make sure it was green.

RAY
Green?

JILLIA
I'd pruned the poplar in our front yard early in the spring. I had three vases and I stuffed the bare branches in water. They budded

and leafed out in his room.

One vase sat on his window sill. When I'd approach the hospital, I'd see how Elijah's window shone. And I knew that even for a moment we were both seeing the same green leaves. Of course the poplar leaves fell before fall so I scoured every flower shop in Winnipeg for greenery.

Every afternoon he'd say, "Tell me." He meant I should go to the window, move the vase, sit looking out and tell him what I saw.

I'd often tell him about passersby. A jaunty hat or a brightly coloured scarf. Some days there was no one and I'd make it up just to see him smile.

One day there was a young man walking briskly into the very blustery wind. He slipped on the ice and his greatcoat filled with air. I swear he flew before he fell. Elijah laughed even though it must have hurt. That was the last time I heard his laugh. I won't forget that laugh.

RAY
Nor I Brit's. She had a very unconventional laugh. She was just a wee thing but she guffawed like a sailor. And if she found something especially funny, she'd snort!

JILLIA
I miss so much about Elijah. I miss dancing. I miss wanting to dance.

RAY
I bet your feet still want to dance. May I?

JILLIA
Not here, Ray!

RAY
Fine.

> *He jumps to his feet.*

RAY
Peppermint for the first lady to dance with me in this station.

> *Jillia looks around then quickly faces him.*

JILLIA
Sir.

RAY
Miss.

> *They begin to dance in slow circles looking as if they'd been dancing together their whole lives*
>
> *Lights down.*

Scene 4: Honeymoon bed

> *Ray and Jillia are tucked in bed, but we can see they have matching pj tops.*

JILLIA
Imagine a second honeymoon in a year! You do spoil me, Raymond.

RAY
Oh. Do you mind? I could stop.

> *She takes Ray's head in her hands and kisses him deeply.*

JILLIA
Never!
   Did you think you'd ever be this happy?

RAY
Twice in a lifetime? No.

JILLIA
I thought Elijah loving me was a miracle. I was so sure that once he really knew me, he wouldn't like me. He hung in. I told him one day that I didn't deserve a love like ours. He said maybe no one deserves it, but they inspire it in each other.

And now you. So late in my life. At first I worried that we could not match Elijah and me, so why bother. You make me so happy.

RAY
Or together we are so happy! Only one thing could make me happier.

JILLIA
Yes?

RAY
Your feet! I would have them toasty warm!

Do you ever wonder that because you and I found two loves in our respective lifetimes that maybe we deprived two other people of their only love?

JILLIA
Did I ever tell you about the community garden? Elijah's favourite 'tell me' view. I told him what was happening in 'his' garden: the spring planting; the summer weeding; the harvest. Just at the edge of winter a green plastic lawn chair appeared in the garden.

Elijah whispered to me that he would one day soon upright the chair and sit. Just sit. Such a meagre dream but still I knew it could never happen.

A few days later his voice was gone. He wrote on his board, 'Don't want to leave.'

I was already wrapped to the eyeballs against the cold. I told him I didn't have to go. He wrote 'No me!'

I went out to the garden once he'd dozed off. It took a bit of oomph to free the chair and stand it up. I sat. Just sat. I felt heavy, too big for the chair. I stayed maybe 10 minutes. Suddenly, I felt lighter. I knew my Elijah was gone.

RAY
I hope you are never lost to me.

JILLIA
You could always leave a trail of peppermints!

> *Lights down.*

> *Scene 5: The nursing home*

> *Lights up on the curtained bed as in Scene 1. Ray is still sitting in the chair outside the curtain.*

RAY
All the peppermint trails she could ever want and still she is lost to both of us.

JILLIA
Why are you still sitting way over there, you silly man? And to whom are you speaking? Hurry: my feet are cold!
   And I'd like another peppermint. I can't wait to tell you everything. I remember us! Please come to bed, Elijah.

> *Ray takes a ragged sobbing breath.*

RAY
Coming, Jillia. Just getting your peppermint.

> *Lights down.*

> *The end.*

Pam Calabrese MacLean

The inspiration for "Peppermints"

"Peppermints" was conceived while my middle son, Emis, and I were helping my Mother move from her one-bedroom apartment (with a stove) to a studio apartment with no stove. The writing as well as the scorched paint was on the wall.

    I was outside getting some fresh air, which in those days meant I was having a smoke. I noticed an old man walking away from the building that cared for the residents who were next to their final rest. His step was lively but as he came closer, I could see sorrow in his face.

    He leaned against the concrete wall next to me. "Can you spare a cigarette? First in 40 years. Been to see my wife."

    He held out a bag of peppermints and I took one.

    "I go every night. She won't get ready for bed unless I'm there with her peppermint reward. She didn't recognize me tonight. I'll still visit."

    As he walked away he doffed his hat, saying only, "Next time."

-PCM

Pam Calabrese MacLean

Awake

Time
Now

Setting
A funeral parlour, with an open casket. Delia lies in the casket. The foot of the casket is downstage. The head of the casket is elevated slightly so that she can be seen and heard.

There are three chairs at right angles to the head of the casket. There is a small table at the head of the casket for flowers. There are no flowers.

Although Delia speaks, opens and moves her eyes, she resembles a corpse in every other aspect.

Cast

DELIA, a woman in her sixties
ALICE, a street woman of about the same age
Delivery Man, An offstage voice

Pam Calabrese MacLean

Awake

A funeral home. Delia lies in her casket.
Alice, a street woman about the same age as Delia enters and stands next to the casket. She is ragged but clean. She is dressed in layers and is wearing a head scarf. She sets her many bags down by the casket, leans in to get a better look, her face inches from the dead woman's face.

DELIA
You're supposed to say something nice.

Alice jumps back with a muffled scream.

DELIA
I'm dead.

Alice turns and heads for the exit.

DELIA
And you're quick!

Alice hesitates but does not turn back toward the casket.

DELIA
Wait! Your bags.

Alice turns and cautiously approaches the casket, looking for evidence of a trick.
Delia takes a good look at Alice.

DELIA
Do I know you?

ALICE
No.

DELIA
(big sigh)
Good.

ALICE
Why?

DELIA
Could be another cruel trick of death. Waiting for a bunch of people to tell say nice things about you, but you don't recognize one face. Not one story.

ALICE
You can't hear them anyway.

DELIA
I can hear you.

> *Alice picks up her bags, backs to the chair farthest from the coffin. Remains standing, clutching her bags.*

DELIA
Why are you here? Dead too?

ALICE
Dead tired.

DELIA
I thought death would be different.

ALICE
I thought death would be quieter.

DELIA
Different from my life.

ALICE
Isn't it?

DELIA
Not much. I'm still waiting. I'm still angry. Disappointed.

ALICE
(quitely as a sigh)
Bitter. Lonely.

DELIA
Say something. I'm bored.

Slight pause. We see the light of an idea in her face.

ALICE
How did you know you were dead?

DELIA
Good question! Now we're getting somewhere!

ALICE
I might be getting somewhere!

DELIA
I was getting ready for my hair appointment.

ALICE
It looks good. Who does it?

DELIA
I was hurrying. Every time I looked at the clock it was 8:10.

ALICE
It's been ages since I had my hair done.

DELIA
I looked out the window. Traffic was stopped. A man stood, mid-stride, a cigarette two inches from his lips.

ALICE
A cigarette would be good right now.

DELIA
A dog was peeing on a post. Not even the stream was moving.

ALICE
You die, and it all stops? You cross over, it all starts again? Is that what you're telling me? What about here? What about me?

DELIA
I think this place is some kind of terminal.

ALICE
And the dead exit one way and the living…

DELIA
Never mind. If you believe the brochure I'll be alive somewhere else soon!

Alice circles her finger beside her head, indicating Delia is crazy.

ALICE
Dead woman talking!

SOUND: Crowd of people offstage.
Alice turns towards the noise.

ALICE
I better get out of here. Before some—

DELIA
There won't be anyone.

ALICE
No one?

DELIA
There are only three damned chairs. All they could spare from Mr. look-how-many-people-love-me across the hall. All day sobbing and weeping and flowers, flowers, flowers!
   Is he any more dead than I am?

ALICE
God, I hope so!

DELIA
See all the chairs he's got. Hardly room for all those people!

Alice shifts in her seat. Delia looks at her suspiciously.

DELIA
You're overflow!

ALICE
(offended)
I am not! You're awful suspicious for someone not much else can happen to.
   Do you really think if you had a lot of chairs more people would come?

DELIA
You have enough of anything, people want it. Think they can't live without it. Ever been to Wal-Mart?

ALICE
This is different.
   What's your name?

DELIA
It's on the book at the door. Least you could do is sign!

ALICE
You do that on the way out.

DELIA
My name's Delia.
(sing-song voice)
      Delia's my flower
      My flower
      My flower

ALICE
Wouldn't that be dahlia?

DELIA
(beginning to cry)
That's what Rose used to call me.

ALICE
You're crying. I'm pretty sure the dead can't do that.

DELIA
Ever been dead?

Alice takes a one-ounce liquor bottle from her purse, takes a sip.

ALICE
Want some?

DELIA
I'm DEAD!

ALICE
Make up your mind. You can cry but you can't drink. Stick to the rules.

DELIA
I'll have to pick up a copy of those next time I'm out!

Long pause.

DELIA
You want to know what I think?

ALICE
I want to get back to the chairs, the Wal-Mart thing. It's different. People don't walk by a funeral home on a Friday night, look in, see all the chairs and think, "Oh, I have to be there."

DELIA
Want to know how I died?

ALICE
I know that already.

DELIA
You do?

ALICE
There are as many deaths out there as there are living things. You live until you come face to face with your very own. Fits like a shroud.

DELIA
Sounds deep. But it's stupid. You just said that you live 'til you die. Like the sampler my sister Rose embroidered...

ALICE
What did it say?
   Wait. You have a sister?

Delia grunts dismissively.

ALICE
What do you mean by that?

DELIA
You? Family?

Alice grunts dismissively in a tone that echoes Delia's..

DELIA
That's what I mean by that!

ALICE
I'm here to tell you that having a lot of chairs isn't going to lure people. Who do you want to come?

DELIA
Tell me something about you.

ALICE
My name's Alice.

Long pause.

DELIA
That's all I get?

ALICE
What difference does it make?

DELIA
Humour me. I'm trying to change.

ALICE
Little late, don't you think?

DELIA
Are you a good woman, Alice?

ALICE
Depends who you talk to!

DELIA
Will you have a wake room full?

ALICE
I hope my children will forgive me and come.

DELIA
Not your husband?

ALICE
You're awfully nosy for a corpse.

DELIA
Alice, everything we're ever going to learn from each other, we have to learn right now.

ALICE
What makes you think you have anything to teach me?
   I'm tired.

DELIA
But not dead.

ALICE
Okay, you answer my question. Then I'll answer yours.

DELIA
What was your question again?

ALICE
Who do you want at your wake?

DELIA
People.

ALICE
You like people?

DELIA
Christ, no! They're stupid!

ALICE
Lucky you. You never have to deal with them again.

DELIA
It is heaven!

ALICE
But you want a room full? There's no one in particular you'd like to see wiping away a little tear?

DELIA
For sure not my sister.

ALICE
Delia, if this is a Rite of Passage, you better get on with it.

DELIA
What do you mean, Rite of Passage?

ALICE
You know. Before you can cross over you have to make one person love you or understand you. Or stay in the room with you for longer than 10 minutes!

DELIA
Maybe it's your Rite of Passage, Alice.

ALICE
You died so I can turn my life around?
    Delia, this is something you need to do. Believe it or not, your death is about you, not me.
    I want you to imagine a house. Build it board by board. Finish the floors. Pick out the curtains. Sit back. Look around.
    Who do you want to drop by? Who would you invite in?

DELIA
I can't think of a living soul.

ALICE
Me either.
    I'd want my husband but...

DELIA
So you *can* think of a living soul?

ALICE
Not a living soul.

DELIA
Oh, Alice.
    You know what survives the dead? Thirst, hunger, the appetite

for living. They pass it on. Fill other people's lives with their longing.

ALICE
Then my whole life has been full of his longing. It's pushed everything, everyone out.
   There's no one.

DELIA
Not your kids, Alice?

ALICE
Pushed them out hardest of all. I wasn't going to take a chance. By the time I changed my mind, they were long gone.
   You can only take so much of someone else's sadness.

DELIA
I'm sorry, Alice, I wish I could let you talk. I don't think I have much time.
   Something other than your aching feet got you in here. I wanted you to come. And you did.

ALICE
No one's dying wish is for some depressed, cranky, old woman to come to their wake.

DELIA
I didn't want be alone. I'm frightened.

ALICE
Well, I'm here.

   Alice goes to the coffin, reaches in and pats Delia's hand.

DELIA
Will you stay until...I'm gone?

Alice is a little overwhelmed but tries to joke.

ALICE
Only if you tell me what was on that sampler?

DELIA
That which doesn't kill you...

ALICE
Makes you stronger?

DELIA
Nope...keeps you going until something else does.

ALICE
That is stupidly profound.

DELIA
Don't be one of those, Alice. Wake up. You still have time.

DELIVERY MAN
(off stage)
I've got flowers...

ALICE
In here!
(to Delia)
I'll be right back.

> *Alice steps into the hall and returns with a floral arrangement. She removes and reads the card, then tosses the card over her shoulder. She places the flowers on the table.*

DELIA
For me?

Pam Calabrese MacLean

ALICE
They are now!

Lights down.

The end.

About "Awake"

I hadn't really thought about death until, at age eight, I was returning from vacation with my parents. I waited for my dog, Perky, to appear and run three times around the house - one round for each of us whether we were gone ten minutes or days.

I had yet to be told that Perky had been hit by a car. Perky was dead. I had so many questions.

Where is he?
Does he know he's dead?
Does he wonder about me?
What about thirst, hunger?
Is he frightened? If yes, of what?
Does he remember pats and scratches?
Does he still love me?
No one seemed to have any answers.

When my Dad was burned to death, I was 16, and the questions took on an urgency.

"Awake" and much of my poetry are attempts to find answers.

-PCM

Pam Calabrese MacLean

Wanna Bet?

Time
Now

Setting
A casino lounge. A fancy couch and armchair at right angles to each other. The chair is SR of the couch. They share a corner table and a lamp. There are three fancy arrow signs on the wall above the couch: the arrow pointing up with symbol for stairs says BAR and GRILL; the stage right arrow says AIRPORT LIMOUSINE; the stage left says CASINO.

Cast

Charlotte, an elderly woman. She is well dressed but her clothes are old and out of fashion. She is a bit of a smart ass.
Marsha, a woman in her 50s.

Pam Calabrese MacLean

Wanna Bet?

> *SOUND: Casino sounds*
> *Lights up on a casino lounge. CHARLOTTE is sitting in the armchair. She looks conflicted.*
>   *MARSHA ENTERS SR from the airport limousine. She has a coffee in hand. She is jittery She tries hard to keep a wall of anger between Char and herself. Stands looking towards the exit to the airport limo.*

CHARLOTTE
Hello.

> *Beat.*

CHARLOTTE
(louder)
Hello!

> *Another beat.*

CHARLOTTE
Hey you!

> *Another beat.*

CHARLOTTE
Lady Jitterbug! Saint Vitus' dance partner.

MARSHA
You talking to me?

Charlotte takes an exaggerated look around.

CHARLOTTE
Yep. Thin pickings!
   He's patron Saint of actors, dancers and people who drink too much coffee.

MARSHA
Who?

CHARLOTTE
Saint Vitus.

MARSHA
It's decaf!

CHARLOTTE
Waste of a swallow in my books. Like non-alcoholic beer. Call it what it is: beer-flavoured pop.

MARSHA
You sure make a person want to sit and chat!

CHARLOTTE
You're being fastidious, right?

MARSHA
Facetious.

CHARLOTTE
Always got those two confused.

MARSHA
Conversation killer!

CHARLOTTE
Sit down & breathe in a little life.

MARSHA
Talk about your lack of vocabulary?

CHARLOTTE
You can't know what I know from one mistook word.

MARSHA
Mistook?

CHARLOTTE
You come in the limo? You came in the limo entrance.

Marsha gives her a withering look.

CHARLOTTE
Just making small talk.

MARSHA
I don't do small talk.

CHARLOTTE
Makes a better conversation with two. C'mon. Try it. You might like it!

Marsha sits as far from Charlotte as possible.

MARSHA
Why are you here?

CHARLOTTE
Assuming that's not a deep philosophical question, I'd have to say just lucky.

MARSHA
Meeting someone?

CHARLOTTE
"Two reasons why people don't mind their own business. No mind and no business!"

MARSHA
I thought you wanted small talk. You here to annoy us innocent passers-by?

CHARLOTTE
You didn't pass by!

MARSHA
You here to gamble?

CHARLOTTE
My age—every day is a gamble!

MARSHA
I'm trying my best here. I don't work for *Frank* Magazine. Just curious.

CHARLOTTE
Ever notice that if you like someone, you say they're curious? But if you don't like them, they're nosy. You're nosy!

MARSHA
You're infuriating! You want me to talk. Then you don't want me to talk. I get to spill my guts and get nothing in return?

CHARLOTTE
Pretty much! Don't want to share? Fine by me. I've heard so so many tales of woe! Too many for one woman in one short lifetime!

MARSHA
Not short enough.

CHARLOTTE
You don't like me. I can live with that.

MARSHA
I am so relieved!

CHARLOTTE
So what is your sad story?

MARSHA
Don't have one.

CHARLOTTE
Every addict's got one.

MARSHA
Not an addict! I don't smoke, drink or do drugs.

CHARLOTTE
A one-vice wonder! If you're a gambler you're an addict.

MARSHA
I'm not a gambler.

CHARLOTTE
You're a gambler.

MARSHA
Want to bet?

CHARLOTTE
I love sure things!
    Doing well in there?

MARSHA
Fifty bucks short of my...goal.

CHARLOTTE
Gotcha. Gambler.

MARSHA
Not fair. You saw me in there.

She points to Casino entrance.

CHARLOTTE
No.

She points two fingers at Marsha's eyes.

CHARLOTTE
I saw you in there!

MARSHA
In my eyes...You are bat-shit crazy!

CHARLOTTE
I can spot a gambler!

MARSHA
I can spot a loser!

CHARLOTTE
Mirror mirror?

MARSHA
Now you're just being fucking ignorant!

CHARLOTTE
Oh, look at you, all umbraged!

MARSHA
Umbraged?

CHARLOTTE
You got your back up and you think the barbs can't get to you.

MARSHA
Your name Barb?

CHARLOTTE
No. Charlotte. My old man called me Charlottery—not with a great deal of affection. Said my number would come up.

MARSHA
(Nervously)
Past tense?

CHARLOTTE
His num—

MARSHA
Not listening!

CHARLOTTE
High dungeon, is it?

MARSHA
Dudgeon!

CHARLOTTE
So you *are* listening. His number came up. Tits up and balls to the breeze. At least I know where to find him.

MARSHA
That's disgusting.

    Beat.

CHARLOTTE
You mentioned a goal.

MARSHA
A plane ticket.

CHARLOTTE
Going somewhere?

MARSHA
No I just want to buy a ticket so I can shred it.

CHARLOTTE
Stupid question. Where are you going?

MARSHA
Am I being investigated?

CHARLOTTE
Why? What have you done?

MARSHA
Nothing.

CHARLOTTE
Sometimes it's easier to talk about the hard stuff to a stranger.

MARSHA
Don't come much stranger than you.

But she looks thoughtfully at Charlotte and takes a deep breath.

MARSHA
I want to say I'm done. I want to believe I'm done. I want to be done.

CHARLOTTE
With small talk?

MARSHA
Gambling!

CHARLOTTE
So say it already.

MARSHA
No.

CHARLOTTE
Not your first cattle drive?

MARSHA
What?

CHARLOTTE
Not the first time you believed you were done.

MARSHA
OMG you are a gambler, too. Lose it all?

CHARLOTTE
Not today.

Marsha
You won big?

CHARLOTTE
Where?

MARSHA
In there.

CHARLOTTE
In there?

MARSHA
In the casino.

CHARLOTTE
Never big enough.

MARSHA
You're hurting my head.

CHARLOTTE
Why suffer alone?

MARSHA
Luck's got to change eventually, right?

CHARLOTTE
Not that I've noticed.

MARSHA
Bit of a bummer, aren't you?

CHARLOTTE
A realist.

MARSHA
I'm glad I don't share your reality.

CHARLOTTE
Just because you see it differently, doesn't make it different.

MARSHA
You sure about that?

CHARLOTTE
In there...

She points to the casino.

CHARLOTTE
That's hell.

MARSHA
Heaven to some.

CHARLOTTE
Don't change what it is. A Casino.

MARSHA
What are you? Some travelling black cloud?

CHARLOTTE
Looks of you, I'm not the black cloud took the shine off your day!

MARSHA
I'll have you know that this is me happy.

CHARLOTTE
Hope I never see you miserable.

MARSHA
I'm buying a ticket and I'm getting on that plane. There's a lot at stake.

CHARLOTTE
More than last time?

MARSHA
How do you know there WAS a last time?

Charlotte raises her eyebrows.

MARSHA
My last chance.

CHARLOTTE
Says who?

MARSHA
My husband.

CHARLOTTE
You got kids?

Marsha
Not anymore.

CHARLOTTE
Gambled them away?

MARSHA
Closer to the truth than you know.

CHARLOTTE
How old?

MARSHA
Why do you care?

CHARLOTTE
Trying to help.

MARSHA
Did I say I had a problem? Needed help?

CHARLOTTE
Not in so many words.

MARSHA
Now you're a mind-reader?

CHARLOTTE
Let's say I got a keen sense of impending disaster.

MARSHA
I'm a disaster?

CHARLOTTE
Standing on the edge.

MARSHA
You going to catch me?

CHARLOTTE
Always thought I'd make a good counsellor.

MARSHA
How'd that work out for you?

CHARLOTTE
Where's hubby and kids now?

MARSHA
Toronto.

CHARLOTTE
How old?

MARSHA
Almost 50. Why? You a cougar?

She laughs at her own joke.

CHARLOTTE
Ha ha. The kids.

MARSHA
A boy, seven. Twin girls, five.

CHARLOTTE
Still got time, then.

MARSHA
Seven and five last time I saw them. Thirteen and eleven now.
　Last time I saw them I was still living with them. My son made me a calendar. I got a star for every day I didn't gamble. If I made a whole week I'd get a surprise. Never did get a surprise.

CHARLOTTE
Surprise! Surprise!

MARSHA
I'm offering you a job with sex and travel—as in go fuck yourself.
　I stayed with my family for a month but I couldn't take the look in his eyes.

CHARLOTTE
That where you're headed?

MARSHA
I guess.

CHARLOTTE
Here's me blown away by your certainty!

MARSHA
Been headed there before, haven't I?

CHARLOTTE
What stopped you?

MARSHA
None of your business.

CHARLOTTE
But your ex brought the kids to see you?

MARSHA
No. Seems I didn't want it bad enough.

CHARLOTTE
You didn't? You don't?

MARSHA
I think I do. But it's not in my face like gambling.

CHARLOTTE
If you had enough for the ticket, would you go?

MARSHA
He sent me a ticket five years ago.

CHARLOTTE
Really?

MARSHA
No, I just wanted to see if I could make that do-gooder heart of yours beat a little faster.

CHARLOTTE
I get my thrills where I can.

MARSHA
He sent it. I cashed it in, gambled it out.
    How long since you gambled?

Charlotte turns to Marsh in surprise.

CHARLOTTE
No matter how long, it's too long.

MARSHA
I don't know if I can stop.

CHARLOTTE
Gambling's like fighting for peace. Or screwing for virginity. You're feeding what you're trying to starve.

MARSHA
I want my ex to see me as a winner.

CHARLOTTE
He won't. You aren't.

MARSHA
Jesus! That part of your counselling technique? Losers, you're all losers!

CHARLOTTE
You have to admit you have a problem.

MARSHA
So I should lie down, play dead and wait for the vultures!

CHARLOTTE
What could they take that you haven't already lost?

MARSHA
My self-esteem. I have very high self-esteem.

CHARLOTTE
So many people, so much undeserved high esteem!

MARSHA
Being this close to a casino turns you into a right old bitch!

CHARLOTTE
I have to be to do battle.

MARSHA
I don't believe it's a battle I can win. I know you say you've won but you're not dead yet.

CHARLOTTE
Gambling's unsquenchable?

MARSHA
Good word.

CHARLOTTE
I made it up.

MARSHA
I know.

CHARLOTTE
Seems you got something else chasing your tail.

MARSHA
He sent another ticket, Sherlock. Last week. Says if I don't make it there this time—

CHARLOTTE
You'll never find them.

MARSHA
How do you know that?

CHARLOTTE
Part of my fortune telling talent.
    Why are you in there gambling when you already have the ticket?

Long beat.

CHARLOTTE
You lost it. Again.

MARSHA
Why did you ask if you already know?

CHARLOTTE
You're not getting this, are you?

MARSHA
No, you're not getting it. It feels good in there. Like I'm someone in control of their life.

CHARLOTTE
It's not a plane ticket you're gambling.

MARSHA
I hate that he can control me with money.

CHARLOTTE
Oh, sure, all his fault. Your life belongs to him. Is that what you tell yourself when you start to itch?

MARSHA
You don't know me. I stopped for years. My life was empty.

CHARLOTTE
Years?

MARSHA
Two is years.

CHARLOTTE
Why didn't you go home then?

Marsha deflates.

CHARLOTTE
How did it feel, gambling again?

MARSHA
More joy than anything in my life up to that point.

CHARLOTTE
More joy than your kids?

MARSHA
I've been gambling their whole lives, so hard to tell.

CHARLOTTE
Don't you think they deserve the chance?

MARSHA
To give me joy?

CHARLOTTE
No no. That's up to you. It's there but you gotta dig.

MARSHA
Dig, Jesus. Is that what preaching redemption does for you?

CHARLOTTE
My life is empty. I waited too long. I like to think I might get to someone before it's too late for them.

MARSHA
Oh, you're getting to me! What do you think you're offering me?

CHARLOTTE
A chance not to lose your family,

MARSHA
What's your track record with these chances?

CHARLOTTE
Pathetic.

MARSHA
But you keep on. You must have faith in what you're doing.

CHARLOTTE
Faith is believing in what you hope for. I read that on one of those inspirational plaques.

MARSHA
I read one that says try not to let some old woman make you woof your cookies!

CHARLOTTE
So you don't even want to try to quit? It will feel good! I imagine.

MARSHA
There's nothing more righteous than a reformed—
(almost says "whore")
—hooker!

CHARLOTTE
What if I gave you the money?

MARSHA
Old fool losing her mind!

CHARLOTTE
Not that much younger fool losing it all!

MARSHA
You would give me the money why?

CHARLOTTE
So I don't feel like my whole day was a lie.

MARSHA
Isn't that what do-gooders are all about?

CHARLOTTE
Believe me I'm no do-gooder!

MARSHA
I don't want your money.

CHARLOTTE
Because you don't want it or because you'll lose your reason to go back in there? Why don't you pack your bag—

MARSHA
Nothing to pack.

CHARLOTTE
You could check-out—

MARSHA
They're not that formal over the hot air vent.

CHARLOTTE
(fake sympathy)
Ah muffin! God, woman! I'll be dead before you stop lying to yourself!
    I'll cover your shortfall and enough for the limo to the airport.

MARSHA
I don't know.

CHARLOTTE
What? Not a gambler?

MARSHA
It seems so impossible. I'm weak.

CHARLOTTE
Believe me, it's possible.

MARSHA
Everything's possible if you're not the one who has to do it!

CHARLOTTE
That'd make a good plaque! If my life belonged to someone else, I'd know exactly what to do!

MARSHA
And I'm pretty sure you wouldn't shut up about it!

Sofa

CHARLOTTE
Let me do this. Go to your family.

MARSHA
You going to yours?

CHARLOTTE
I'd be a real hypocrite if I wasn't.

MARSHA
What if they don't want me?

CHARLOTTE
You can always go back to gambling!

MARSHA
What if I gamble the money you give me?

CHARLOTTE
Totally your call.

MARSHA
What do you get in return?

CHARLOTTE
Why did you come out of the casino when you were only $50 short?

MARSHA
I felt like I was going to lose.

CHARLOTTE
So you don't want to be some old woman with nothing, no one?

MARSHA
You're an old woman and you're going to tell me you have

something or someone because you quit, right?

CHARLOTTE
No, I'm gonna tell you, you might never get this chance again.

   Beat.

CHARLOTTE
You know I'm pretty sure I'm a Gramma but I'll never know. Don't be like me—never knowing.
   If you were half as hard-ass determined to quit gambling as you are to refuse the money...Buy a ticket. Go home.

   Charlotte opens her purse and pulls out a wad of bills & stuffs them into Marsha's bag.

MARSHA
I promise you—

CHARLOTTE
Don't promise me. Promise you!.

   After an uncomfortable silence, Marsha EXITS toward the airport limousine. Charlotte watches her go, then turns and heads for the Casino. She pauses and looks over her shoulder after Marsha.

CHARLOTTE Oh, what a hypocrite I am!

   She EXITS toward the Casino.
   Lights out.

The end.

About "Wanna bet?"

I was sitting in the lobby of a hotel that housed a Casino on its top floor. Two women were coming down the stairs, arguing. People started to stare. I moved closer to hear better.

They were arguing which of them was the gambling addict. Neither woman thought *she* had a problem. Both raised their purses as if to strike, but instead separated, went in opposite directions in a mutual huff.

Still within hearing distance one woman shouted, "You'll be back first!"

"Wanna bet?" was the reply.

Within the hour, one of the women came in from outside, looked furtively in all directions, then slipped up the stairs. Another ten minutes and the second woman entered the lobby.

She headed right for the stairs and walked up trying to see behind, ahead and either side of herself at the same time.

-PCM

Pam Calabrese MacLean

Who Knew?

Time
Now

Setting
A living room. The pull out couch SL is still out and unmade. There are two cameras on poles aimed at the couch. Both cameras have lampshades on them—a mostly-failed attempt to hide them. There is a small, over-stocked bar. The door to the world is SR.

Cast

Glory, a woman in her 60s. She is wearing a t-shirt, work pants and a man's sweater with leather at the elbows.
Astrid, a woman in her 60s. She is wearing a dress, a buttoned up cardigan and sensible shoes.

Pam Calabrese MacLean

Who Knew?

An unkempt living room. GLORY is standing by the bar, looking SR toward the door. She has a large drink in her hand.

SOUND: Car door slams, car horn honks, door to outside opens then closes.

ASTRID ENTERS SR from outdoors.

ASTRID
Grrrrrr. That's four for four. Why did I let you talk me into this? Try online dating indeed!

GLORY
Need I remind you? You need to stay in Canada. Not getting any younger, are we? Besides, I did all the work! You wouldn't know a mouse from a motherboard!

ASTRID
I should be on a Christian site.

GLORY
You're not a Christian.

ASTRID
What kind of husband can I expect to find on 'Pots of Flesh'!

GLORY
One who knows he is not getting any unless he marries you. And

who can still perform! You need to provide the government with proof of a real marriage, sex and all!

ASTRID
Are you sure about that?

GLORY
Trust me! I wrote it down somewhere. By the phone I think.

Glory moves to the phone table, picks up a note and reads.

GLORY
Right here. Criteria bla bla bla evidence of valid marriage or same-sex partnership; or evidence of common-law marriage status or conjugal partner status.

ASTRID
They used to believe you on the face of it.

GLORY
Just switched ends! That Kenney dude wants to crack down on marriage fraud.

ASTRID
Right, you now have to live with your sponsor for two years after the marriage. That's longer than most couples last these days!

GLORY
And they interview you, your neighbours and friends. They watch you.

ASTRID
I don't know if I could handle living with a man for two years after my life with Charlie.

GLORY
I can't imagine one night after my years with Milly.

Pause for thought.

GLORY
I have an idea.

ASTRID
No more men!

GLORY
Exactly. A woman. And no waiting another year.
(sings ditty)
Don't wait for spring do it now, when there are girls who know how! If the job is interior the work'll be superior. So why wait…?

ASTRID
I only have a month to meet someone, fall in…well whatever you fall in at our age. Besides. you know I'm poker straight!

GLORY
You can bend without breaking.

ASTRID
Do you think you were born a lesbian? Can it overtake you later in life?

GLORY
Like the plague?

ASTRID
That's why Gertie next door won't come in for a drink. Thinks it's contagious.

GLORY
Is that really why she doesn't come over?
   I've tried men. I told you that before.

ASTRID
Trying isn't buying.

GLORY
It should be! Then you could return them! They were pretty disastrous. You should try a woman! You might be surprised!

ASTRID
Just because you did a couple of men? You want to level the playing field so I can suffer in equal measure? Not only do I not know the difference between a mouse and a motherboard—

GLORY
You are not going to tell me that you don't know an um from a—

ASTRID
Can we drop this, please?

GLORY
Okay. So what was this one's excuse?

ASTRID
Apparently he'd forgotten he was married until today when I said no hanky-panky until the knot is tied.

GLORY
Convenient. Maybe he couldn't do it anyway.

ASTRID
Going by what he handed me under the table, he still can. He was looking for an hour of sex a month! I asked how many times we'd need to meet to get an hour!

GLORY
Did he get it?

ASTRID
No, and not the joke either?

GLORY
You got a free meal and a hand out!

ASTRID
Glory! And for your edification he walked out and left me the bill.

GLORY
Dare I say stiffed you? Didn't you pay last time because #3 said the date was your idea? A lot of stiffing for someone who's not getting any.

ASTRID
Only stiff one I want is the one in your glass.

> *Glory goes to the bar and makes a Scotch on the rocks while they talk. She tops up her own drink.*

GLORY
At least he drove you home.

ASTRID
No. A cab. Why can't I find another Charlie? Or a reasonable facsimile? Even an unreasonable one!

GLORY
Yes. I'll have a Scotch on the rocks. And another Milly, please.

ASTRID
You're the only person I love as much as Charlie.

> *Glory hands Astrid her drink, takes her own and sits on the pull-out bed.*

GLORY
Ditto. Maybe I'm the woman you should try?

ASTRID
Please change the subject, you old lesbo!

> *Glory pats the pull-out bed beside her in an inviting way. Astrid doesn't move.*

GLORY
Let's review your post-Charlie experiences with men.

ASTRID
Let's not.

GLORY
Oh good. So you are ready to try a woman. Just not me, right?

> *Pause. Astrid stands, moves over to the bed and sits besie Glory.*

ASTRID
Let's review.

GLORY
There was van-guy and his pink plush shag wagon. Half an hour every second Friday while his wife had her hair done. Or no shag as it turned out! There was the Kenny Rogers look alike. And Mister 'oh yes I'd like you to meet my homicidal ex'!

ASTRID
Who didn't know she was an 'ex'. What about the guy who had his

apartment decorated with pictures of his dead wife?

GLORY
I'm not sure I remember that one.

ASTRID
Oh I'm sure you do. Her bosom was so formidable that all the photos had to be 'landscape'! I was pleasantly surprised that her husband included her head!
    Enough with the nightmare memories. I didn't want intimacy with any of them.

GLORY
How long do we have to figure something out?

ASTRID
Not long enough.

GLORY
I wish your health was better. Hard to imagine you making the trek another year. You were exhausted for weeks after you got here.

ASTRID
Remember how proud Charlie was to take the three girls out for an evening.

GLORY
People made so many assumptions. All wrong. But amusing.

ASTRID
Well Charlie introducing us as 'Meet my wife, my ex and my mistress!' didn't help.
    Where's the big picture of the four of us?

GLORY
It fell. I'm getting the frame fixed and new glass.

ASTRID
Right, Milly made that frame.

GLORY
I have the picture in the big book by my desk. The frame will be back before you are. I'm so afraid you won't be coming again.

ASTRID
I'm afraid too. I can't lose you.

GLORY
Do you regret not having a kid?

ASTRID
I do now. A little piece of Charlie would be nice.

GLORY
We didn't have a hope in Hell to adopt back then. We wanted to. Milly a little more than me.

ASTRID
I was pregnant once.

GLORY
I didn't know.

ASTRID
I didn't want to get rid of the baby but neither of us wanted to raise a child. I had parents so in love that my sister and I were raised by benign neglect!
    My parents were selfish. They didn't want to share one other. Charlie and I were the same. Charlie said we should give her to you and Milly.

GLORY
A girl? You'd trust her to us? Not worried she'd catch the lesbian

disease?

ASTRID
We were all set to tell you and Milly got sick. And I miscarried.

GLORY
You could have told us anyway.

ASTRID
Charlie did tell Milly. She asked that we not tell you. I thought maybe she wanted to be the one.

GLORY
Then she was gone.

ASTRID
Maybe she thought it would be cruel for us to wave your dream in front of you. Then destroy it in the same breath.

GLORY
Maybe she didn't plan on telling me.

ASTRID
What are we going to do?

GLORY
Don't go back. You're not thinking straight.

ASTRID
(exasperated)
Only way I can think!

GLORY
You're not making sense. If you can't even imagine sex with a man other that Charlie, how can you live with one?

ASTRID
I thought I'd marry, go through the motions and, after a respectable time, leave…

GLORY
You're already here. Marry me—we can cut out the middle man.

ASTRID
Marry you! You're my best friend!

GLORY
Which side are you arguing again?

ASTRID
It would change things. If we make love, get married, I'd have to leave you.

GLORY
Why?

ASTRID
It's not natural. Like trying to put two shoes on the same foot.

GLORY
You've always been so accepting of me.

ASTRID
I love you.

GLORY
Yet you'd rather do it with a man you don't love than a woman you do? Now that seems unnatural to me.

ASTRID
I don't think I could even kiss you.

GLORY
You kiss me all the time.
ASTRID
But I don't KISS you!

GLORY
My lips, a man's lips. They're just lips!

ASTRID
You do have other lips!

GLORY
So you do know your mouse from—

ASTRID
Be quiet! And tongues. Besides, we don't have time to get married.

GLORY
If we submit the proof of our sexual relationship, apply for a marriage license. I'll go to Colorado with you. We can come back once we get the good housekeeping seal of approval.

> SOUND: Doorbell rings.
> Astrid goes to the door and talks as she returns with a letter.

ASTRID
What if it destroys our friendship?

GLORY
Who even writes letters these days?

ASTRID
(opening the letter)
My landlord, apparently.

GLORY
Astrid, have you never considered making love to me?

> *Astrid bursts into tears.*

GLORY
No! No! If you hate it I promise I will never—

ASTRID
It's not that. My apartment building burned—

> *Glory goes to her, pulls her close. Astrid sobs, then pulls away.*

ASTRID
To the ground, Glory. To the ground.

GLORY
You lost everything?

ASTRID
Where will I live, Glory?

GLORY
All the more reason to marry me and live here.

ASTRID
It could still ruin things.

GLORY
Can it be worse than going back to no-one and nothing? You're not making any sense.

> *Astrid begins to cry again and Glory draws her into her arms.*

GLORY
Be sensible.

ASTRID
Who's not being sensible? I have some ideas how a man and a woman prove their sex life, but...

> *Glory uncovers the cameras mounted in the corner and aimed at the pull-out couch.*

ASTRID
How long have you been planning this?

GLORY
After the first two duds you tried.

ASTRID
Why two cameras?

GLORY
Non-stop random stills.

ASTRID
Well, there better be film!

GLORY
Trust me!

ASTRID
Said the spider to the fly!

> *Glory offers her hand to Astrid. They attempt a kiss. Astrid manages to put as much distance as possible between them, meeting only at the lips and holding both Glory's hands, more to keep them off her than in affection.*

GLORY
Relax. Not like Hell. Won't last forever.

ASTRID
Is the camera on?

GLORY
Thought I'd wait a bit. At least until you stop looking like you're about to kiss the bubonic plague!

ASTRID
Let's start again.

> *Astrid puts her arms around Glory as far from her butt as possible.*

ASTRID
Pucker up. I'm ready.

GLORY
Did you just suck a lemon?

ASTRID
I can't do this!
   Is it okay if I pretend you're Charlie?

GLORY
Yes, kiss me like you kissed him.

ASTRID
I'll get it this time.

> *They move in for the kiss. Glory reaches for the top button on Astrid's cardigan. Astrid jumps.*

GLORY
You can't jump away.

ASTRID
Yes I can. I just did!

> *Slowly they manage a very romantic kiss. Astrid groans and jumps back again.*

GLORY
It's all right, you know.

ASTRID
I'm pretty sure it shouldn't make me feel like that!

> *They kiss again, longer and deeper. Astrid fits her body to Glory's. Glory hold Astrid's face in her hands. They continue the kiss as Glory gently steers Astrid towards the couch.*

ASTRID
Turn the cameras on! This is your one and only chance!

> *Glory picks up a remote control and clicks. She begins to unbutton Astrid's sweater. The backs of her hands almost touching Astrid's breasts.*

GLORY
You're shivering. Turn around and let me unzip you. Then scoot under the blankets.

ASTRID
Can we dim the lights? Will it be too dark for the cameras?

> *Glory claps her hands and the LIGHTS DIM.*
> *Astrid turns and Glory unzips the dress and slips it off to reveal a lovely slip. Astrid dives under the covers. Glory strips down to a t-shirt and boxer shorts. She joins Astrid in bed.*
> *They look at each other from opposite pillows and kiss again. Together they pull the covers over their heads.*

There is a lot of commotion and soft sounds from under the sheet.
Camera flashes revealing them in a different position. This is playfully done to balance the kiss.
Less commotion and the sounds have softened.
Final camera flash to reveal Astrid spooned against Glory. Next flash Astrid lifts her head and faces the audience.

ASTRID
Who knew!

Last flash Glory's hand raised.
Lights down.

The end.

A running joke

"Who Knew?" started as a running joke with a friend who lives in the forests of West Virginia. We have been close friends for nearly two decades. Every time he visits the conversation is some variation of this:

HIM
I want to live here but I'm too old. Canada doesn't want another old drain on healthcare!

ME
Just marry me, we'll live together. Hopefully we can stick it out long enough to satisfy immigration. Send a few pics of us gardening, cooking, laughing, loving.

HIM
It would be like sleeping with my sister!

ME
We wouldn't have to do the deed. We wouldn't even need to see each other naked. How would anyone know?

HIM
These days we have to conjugate like two old verbs. And provide proof!

ME
Maybe the government is trying to get into bed with the people.

Pam Calabrese MacLean

HIM
One person is one too many! difficult enough!

ME
It could be more difficult. You could be a woman too!

-PCM

Sunnyside Café

Time
Now

Setting
A restaurant. There is a table with three chairs around it. The table has a red gingham tablecloth.

Cast

Eva, A woman in her fifties.

Note: when Eva speaks as her mother, her voice is raspy and has an Eastern European accent.

Pam Calabrese MacLean

Sunnyside Café

> *EVA, wearing a waitress uniform, ENTERS SR, crosses the stage and EXITS SL.*
>
> *Eva ENTERS SL carrying a tray of salt shakers and an old teapot full of salt. She takes her shoes off and sits before she begins to fill the shakers. Her toes poke through a hole in her pantyhose.*

EVA
This is the last thing I do Saturday night. Fill the salt and peppers. My kind of task, simple. Black and white. No real choices. Well, no real consequences.

Safe. Like walking.

No matter where you go, how far, how often, how fast. If you're walking you always have one foot on the ground.

I like having one foot on the ground.

Surprises me that I loved to dance. But I did. When I was a young woman and if tips were good I'd play the jukebox while I worked and sometimes I'd be done all my jobs and there'd be music leftover and I'd dance.

There was never anyone here but me. No one to lift or twirl me. So really, just fancy walking.

I've lived nearly my whole life 89 steps from the Sunnyside Cafe's front door.

Mama and I came here when I was two weeks old. Some of it I truly remember and some I know is just Mama.

She told how in the beginning, she'd bound me tight, left me to go out and wash other people's dishes, racing home from the Sunnyside Cafe, across Melbourne Street, up the dark stairs to feed and change me. How later she kept me in a wooden crate that her boss, Mr. Frank, she called him, let stand beside the double steel sink.

One of my first memories. The hissing water, the clatter of the dishes and the black lines running up the back of Mama's legs. She'd lift her right foot and rub the back of her left calf with it. Then the other. But always the right foot first.

(in Mama's voice)
"Eases the aching, Eva."

(in her own voice)
That's what Mama told me about one thing or another my whole life. She had a cure for every ache known to womankind. Well, almost.

Carrying me home from the Sunnyside she'd show me the moon.

(in Mama's voice)
"Always where she should be, Eva! Like me, Eva. Like you!"

(in her own voice)
I wish I could remember what she told me the nights there was no moon.

Might have left me a little room to forgive.

We lived just the two of us, in two rooms, two flights above the drug store.

I remember going into the drug store with Mama. Mr. Jordan Fennel owned it. Like his father and his father's father. Always thought people put too much store—no pun—in that kind of thing. Not everything that gets passed down is good.

Mr. Jordan Fennel gave us our rooms when he sold the store. No one to pass it on to.

Mr. Jordan Fennel always gave me a striped candy stick when Mama brought him his clothes. She mended and cleaned them every week. His wife was dead or crippled or something.

Mr. Jordan Fennel looked at Mama like a broody hen eyeing another's eggs.

That's how Mama described married men who ogle. She never seemed to notice when she was getting the once over.

She was lonely.

(in Mama's voice)
"Got so lonely sometimes, Eva, I'd hold my own hand at the bottom of the dishpan and talk dirty!"

(in her own voice)
Mama never seemed to consider any living man a solution. Waiting for something special, I guess.

I must have had a father, but if you listen to Mama, she did it all herself. Only thing she ever said was that he didn't like her soup!

I have so many questions. Is he dead? Did he come to Canada with us? Did we lose him on the way? Did Mama love him? Did he love me?

I could never do that to a child. What Mama did. Keeping it all for herself.

I used to make believe that Mr. Jordan Fennel was my father. He's dead now. Mama's dead and the drug store has been a Laundromat for a long time. And it's just me, living my life over the Duds & Suds.

It's convenient and I don't really mind the smells of other people's lives. When they're clean.

It's a different smell from mine. Lived in.

Not so much waiting.

What is it with waiting anyway? It's not like it's some great virtue. Or some great accomplishment. You just wait.

It's easier than taking a chance.

Mama always said,

(in Mama's voice)
"Wait Eva, wait...things could change, Eva."

(in her own voice)
No, Mama. You have to want to change things. Get out from under

the comfort.

Most of the time I don't know what I'm waiting for. And don't recognize it when it arrives.

Like a flash of pink. Shocking. It disappears. Comes around again. And again.

It was a Sunday evening in the Duds & Suds. Mama did laundry Sunday night. Like it was written in the scripture. Thou shall do thy laundry of a Sunday!

I'm nothing if I'm not Mama's daughter.

These days I sit in the Laundromat on one of those hard plastic chairs and try to read. Usually a book as drab as my laundry. Drab as my life.

Peek out of the corner of my eye. I will not look at it dead on. Mama says

(in Mama's voice)
"if you do that then the thing you're looking at slips away."

(in her own voice)
I don't know what it is or how it made its way into my laundry but I already know I don't want it to disappear.

Years back I used to leave my clothes and trudge up the 37 stairs, watch the café from Mama's favourite chair. Someone stole my clothes. My only dress, two pairs of slacks, one black, one brown, each with a matching twin set. My whole wardrobe.

Well, they left the uniforms. But took my underwear. I can't imagine anyone wanting it.

(in Mama's voice)
"Eva, don't use your underwear to get closer to God!"

(in her own voice)
I get it now. Holey.

My eyes kept drifting to the dryer—brown black drab drab brown drab black. They could have been the exact clothes stolen 25 years earlier. What I was thinking was: Yup, that's about as much has changed in my life!

I watched the clothes tumble to a stop, that split second of hesitation before they fall one after the other burying that sliver of pink.

What if I opened the door and it was gone? I plugged in more dimes. Kept the dryer going until the old guy came to lock up. Nearly fried my uniforms!

I didn't have time to fold anything. Just threw it all in my basket: Seventeen shades of nowhere and one lonely as I am pink sock. A child's. Not as big as the palm of my hand.

Usually when someone misses a sock or a dishcloth, you tack it to the board. Most people here are regulars so it's never long before things get claimed. I didn't do that. I carried my laundry up up up with that pink sock on top. The crowning jewel. A prayer. Didn't even count the steps on my way.

Me – who never puts one foot in front of the other without counting. Me, who knows exactly how many steps from here to anywhere I've ever been.

A whole lot of going nowhere in short numbered steps.

Been counting my way since I was fifteen. You won't get pregnant if you get up and walk around, is what he told me. He drove off, his taillights winking through the trees and I kept walking, one two three—11,827 steps to get back to the Sunnyside.

Evening is my favourite time here. Especially in winter. Day closing down at the same time as the café. Everyone gone home but me. I can slow down. Take my time.

Saturday nights I get to stay later than usual. The once a week jobs added to the daily jobs and I hardly have any home time to fill.

I remember nights I'd be in such a big hurry to play that jukebox and get to the dancing, I'd leave tables with no shakers, double up on others. Even leave some shakers empty.

Morning would show me quick enough what was needed to put things right.

I don't like morning.

I don't like kissing. I thought I would. I tried. His name was Rick. At least that's what it said on the sleeve of his jacket. He came in early morning. Working construction on the other side of Melbourne Street.

He was way too pretty. I flirted. I dared to dream of getting away from Mama. Maybe being a hairdresser.

Took me two weeks to get that kiss. Front seat of his Chevy Malibu. Emptied me out and filled me up at the same time. One kiss.

I remember my bare feet jammed against the driver side window like two dead cod and while he was getting everything he wanted I picked the word Malibu off the glove box. It was just hanging there.

All I got besides pregnant. A bun in the oven and the baker long gone. I still have that word. Malibu.

It was a banner year for me. First and only kiss. Pregnant. First and only friend—Beth Ann.

I met Beth Ann in the park. We were both riding the merry-go-round. I liked to ride the black and white horse. I imagine he strains against the bit, fighting to be free. Each time around tossing his head, missing his chance. It's in his eyes.

Beth Ann likes the seat. She smiles and waves like a grand lady in a fine carriage!

Beth Ann Strickland was one of those stubbornly cheery people. You either love them or you want to smash their face in. Or both

For a while Beth Ann and I met in the park every Sunday afternoon.

I don't like Sunday.

Sunnyside's closed all day. I'm not really supposed to come over. But the Sunnyside is more home than work. Days off undo me. Like storm days when I was a child. My careful habit blown apart. A whole day of uncharted moments.

Sunday, the Sunnyside is a different place. Most everyone knows we're closed. Occasionally someone tries the door or cups their hands between their face and the glass to peer inside. If they catch sight of me, the regulars see me as part and parcel. Strangers hardly see me at all. If they do, I just shake my head, point to the CLOSED sign and they're gone.

Sofa

Peg tried the door once. Right around the time Mama died. Must be close to 20 years ago.

One minute there was nothing but my reflection, the black night behind it, and the next, the oval of Peg's face against the glass. Mama all over again. And me frozen. Not breathing any more than was absolutely needed.

I'd lost track of her. And it weighed on me.

Finding that pink sock lightened me. Let me believe I could have Peg again. At the same time it was so heavy I couldn't lift my foot to take the next step.

I'm here tonight, everything closed around me, waiting for Peg.

Tomorrow is my first Saturday off since Peg was born. Thirty-six years and not one Saturday. Thirty-six years waiting on and waiting for. Never saw my part in it. Never understood the weight of it. The weight of waiting. See Mama, I do have a sense of humour.

I hated Mama for making me such a fine waitress.

Mama washed dishes here for nearly 30 years. She wanted something better for me. Waitress extraordinaire! I've been waiting tables since I was 16.

I have never gone anywhere. Never been on a bus. Never rode a train. Never got farther than where my feet could take me. Only ever been in one car.

That's why I named my daughter Peg. Not short for Margaret. Just Peg. After the winged horse.

I didn't want this for Peg.

"Coffee hot enough? That cream's not off, is it? How do you want those eggs?"

Even when I was thinking, "Why is there always an asshole?" it came out, "Have a great day!"

All those years, waking every morning, believing, 'Today something is going to happen!'

I almost made something happen once. Thought I was ready to try again.

He always sat right here. He was whole-wheat toast, eggs over easy, corn relish with his hash browns, coffee black and his smile opened doors in my skin.

Early morning, Monday to Friday, I could feel him walking long before he crossed Melbourne Street. I'd watch him all the way to the door. Just stop whatever I was doing and stare. What is it about anticipation that makes the reality so sickly?

He had a way of reading his paper that let me know it was okay to talk. Like he was always happy to put aside what he was doing for me.

Mama never liked him.

(in Mama's voice)
"Too charming."

(in her own voice)
A grown up version of Mr. Chevy Malibu.

(in Mama's voice)
"What's a man like that want with a girl like you Eva? One thing!"

(in her own voice)
I should have taken a Saturday off for him!

I went so far as to agree to him picking me up after work. And he came, knocking, pressing his face against the glass.

I watched the snow gather on his shoulders but I never moved. Eventually he went away. Wait long enough, everything goes away.

I sometimes dream him in the doorway, an empty cup in his long, fine fingers. I try to tell him I have nothing to give, but he whispers, "You have everything I need." I step again and again into the possibility of him, but his tongue in my mouth is like Mama said, forked.

I swear by all the soup Mama made, I'm taking tomorrow off. That's why I'm here doing Saturday things on a Friday.

Peg's coming. Here. Tonight.

Eva notices a rip in her uniform. She fingers it.

EVA
Seems I'm coming apart at the seams!
　　Mama would have fixed this while I was on my feet, waiting tables. If I'd let her. A one-woman-wonder! She sewed my clothes, made my lunches out of what she called

(in Mama's voice)
"good folks' leavings."

(in her own voice)
Mama was always making something. Mostly it was to get some time for herself. I was never allowed to interrupt when Mama was working. So it was like she was all alone. She was happy then.
　　I'd be ready to burst and just when I thought I couldn't stay quiet for one more second, she'd set aside whatever she was working on and say,

(in Mama's voice)
"Talk, Eva, talk."

(in her own voice)
I still have the box Mama made me from a box that Mr. Jordan Fennel gave her. It held four bars of soap. Took Mama forever to use it up, but once she did, she covered the box with material from a rag of a dress not even Mama could save. She lined it with a bit of an old silk slip.
　　Sometimes when I open the box I think I can still smell that blue iris soap. But of course that's just foolishness. I keep everything that means something to me in it.
　　It's not a big box.
　　Peg will have it when I'm dead.
　　Mama did everything for me. She saw me off to school, taught me how to cross the street. Showed me how to wear my clothes as if I had a closet full.
　　Mama believed that what you're wearing when you die is what you wear for eternity. No matter how they gussie up the body. And

she believed whatever you've done most of in your life, you just keep on with.
    If that's true, Mama's making soup in a yellow apron with the tiniest blue flowers. She lived making soup.
    Soup every night from bones the butcher saved for a dog we didn't own.

(in Mama's voice)
"Soup to build a life on, Eva."

(in her own voice)
Split pea ham, beef barley, pork potato. Chicken not so often. People bought that with the bone in.
    Mama could have had a whole chicken. And the butcher too. Some of the scraps he saved her said a whole lot more than soup.
    Mama was a charmer. She had an innocent, flirty way about her. And she used it. The butcher, the baker, the candlestick maker— She had them all on a wire. She'd pluck it just as much as was needed to get whatever she thought I had to have. Always me. Never what she might have needed. Wanted.
    Mama believed it was soup Peg needed. Soup that would bring her home. Batch after batch and Mama sure that each one would be THE one that Peg would smell from Wichita or Cheyenne or wherever she was and realize she couldn't live one more day without us.
    I wonder what exactly Beth Ann told Peg about us. Mama and me.
    About the time Peg was five, Mama started setting a place for her.

(in Mama's voice)
"Old enough to be eating late with us Eva!"

(in her own voice)
I washed Peg's dishes, carried them to the cupboard night after night, though she never once used them.

Can't devote yourself to one person like Mama did. Trying to give them what they want before they know they want it.

Some wanting is easy to name. New drapes. A slow cooker. A walk in the park. Some wanting we can't ever name.

Funny how the regulars here are like family and I get into the routine of what they want and just go about doing it. Comfortable.

New customers worry me.

I remember a Saturday morning. Busiest time of the week. The other waitress didn't show. Just me and Frank. He was still alive so I know I was pretty young.

I don't remember peoples' names. I do remember what they eat. What they want from me. She only came in that one time, travelling through, or didn't like the food. Doesn't matter. Eggs benedict, seven grain toast—no butter—and the strongest black coffee we could offer. That's what she said. "Give me the strongest black coffee you can offer."

She didn't speak again until she'd eaten, paid up, pressing a twenty dollar tip on me. Felt sorry, I guess. One little waitress and a café full of hungry people.

She held on to my arm until I had no choice but to look her in the eye. It frightened me that someone could see that far.

"What's your name?"

I reached for my breast pocket —where my nametag should be. Frank wasn't going to be happy if I lost another. It was there. Eva.

"Well, Eva. You watch yourself. Or you're going to wake up one morning and realize you have everything you need, everything you want, and it's not enough."

Now there's a tip I can live without!

Nothing—no thing is ever going to be enough until we allow what we truly want. Some things take up all your wanting room. Like wanting to fill your daughter's bowl, once and once again. And there it is. Said out loud, walking towards you, hand in hand with the possibility that it might be enough.

I was Mama's out-loud wanting. She made a place for me, gave me everything.

I gave my daughter away. Like a fucking puppy.

I couldn't bear to touch her.
Do you want to hold your baby, Eva?
Noooooooooooooooooooooo!
Mama made me.
The baby cried all the time except when Mama was there, holding her. I could see Mama's plan. How she'd use us. An excuse for her own little life.

(in Mama's voice)
"Eva, you can't fill your life up with someone else's living."

(in her own voice)
But isn't that what you're doing, Mama?
  Only time she ever slapped me.
  I understood then. I'd never get away. We'd never get away.
  I kept Peg for five days.
  It wasn't as heartless as it sounds. Not like I handed her over to the first person who walked by. I gave her to my friend. Beth Ann.
  Beth Ann wore an overcoat of cheery. She kept it closed up tight but sometimes I'd catch a glimpse of what ran underneath. Such a sadness. Turns out it all had to do with not being able to carry a baby full term. We met a lot of times, had a lot of talks before I found that out.
  We all have our sad stories. I don't want to hear them. It's that foot in the door thing. I can't let that happen.
  Some stories you hear even when you're working hard not to.
  He ordered dry toast every morning for a week. Never once ate more than a bite. And hot milk.
  After the first morning he timed his arrival so most of the regulars were cleared out. He liked to talk and because I was the only waitress not rushing out back for a smoke, I was the one got talked to.
  I was busy pretending he was my Father coming to find me, waiting for the right moment to call me daughter! So most of what he said I didn't hear.
  I asked him on his last morning what brought him here.

His brother.
I thought that was all he was going to say.
Then he told me. When he was eight, his brother five, they got taken up by different families. Separated for 70 years. His brother lived right here in this town for all of those years and Mr. Hot Milk, Dry Toast lived out west.
Then someone found someone and it was all arranged. Planned out to the second to last detail. Second to last, because they sure hadn't planned the last—his brother getting killed by a car the day before he arrived.
That first day in the café was his brother's funeral. So why are you still here I asked him. He didn't think he could change his ticket.
Three whole days on the bus he said. "We could have had those days if I'd hopped a plane." Time wasted he said.
Try wasting a life time. I could have had all these years with Peg.
I was sixteen and so sure I knew. My decision was white. Blistering white. Like salt.

(in Mama's voice)
"Titch to teaspoon Eva, salt makes the soup!"

(in her own voice)
Salt of the earth. Salt in the wound. It leeched out every bit of colour. Except for that pink sock and the startled blue of Peg's eyes.
Beth Ann came to see the baby and to say goodbye. They were moving. Her husband had a new job. They'd start over.
No they wouldn't try again for a baby.
I told her we should meet in the park the next day. One last get-together.
I packed up everything Mama had sewn for Peg, and while Mama washed dishes across the street, I walked the four blocks over to that park on the corner of Main and Pleasant, kissed Beth Ann on the cheek, and gave her the baby.
My baby.
We didn't stay friends. You can't.

Beth Ann tried. Wrote to me. Fat envelopes that had to have pictures in them.

I didn't open Beth Ann's letters.

I might have kept them except for Mama. It scared me the way she never stopped looking for Peg. Never stopped peering into carriages, playgrounds, other people's lives. She must have taken a billion steps, searching.

More steps than my whole life.

I did see Beth Ann once. Shopping. Just before Christmas the year Peg turned four. I went to the mall. There was Beth Ann, her cart overflowing. Pink. Pink. And more pink. Toys and frills.

She rattled on. They'd moved again. She worked part-time now. Had another baby girl.

Not another. Peg is mine. My baby. Not another.

Beat.

EVA

She won't say Peg and I can't. Like Peg is a bullet to the brain.

They don't call her Peg. Margaret. A dead, dowdy, porridge kind of name. Until Beth Ann says it out loud.

It's all I can hear—a wrap around, a hold you close forever song, an anthem, a prayer answered in a word. Margaret.

Thinking I didn't love Peg was like trying to swallow a fishbone.

All the frilly little outfits are pulsing, rising up—a gaudy, headless merry-go-round circling me. I turn away.

One, two, three. She called my name at fifteen. I didn't slow but I heard. "Eva. Eva! God Damn it Eva, she's happy."

Not me! Not me! I screamed at every passerby. I forgot to count.

Halfway home I knew I was lost. More lost than I'd ever been.

Beat.

EVA

The minute Peg was born, the minute she got that first whiff of the world, you could tell she figured she'd made a mistake.

Sofa

Why did it take me so long?

I handed her over and there was nothing. Not one bit of relief. Just a hole. A 7 pound, 5 ounce hole. I filled my head with numbers so I couldn't feel.

So I wouldn't have to know that all I'd done was trade one fear for another. The fear of never getting away from Mama for the fear of never having Peg. Walking away from Peg...my whole body ached with the weight of her gone.

Walking away takes more steps than walking to.

But I already knew that. I'd been counting my way to the park and home again ever since I knew I was pregnant.

So that day, giving Peg to Beth Ann, I should have been 5,321 steps from home.

When I'd taken every one of the steps. I could see the drug store, the light in our window. I could smell Mama's soup. But I wasn't home.

I could see my life from then on: how I'd pull each day from the one before and that from the one before. Thirty-seven steps down to the street. Fifty-two to cross. Each day kept wooden and falsely bright, achingly the same. But smaller.

Right there, not a hundred steps from the Sunnyside, I had nothing left. I thought I might borrow some steps from tomorrow. But I couldn't start that. God knows where I'd end. So I stood there until way past mid-night.

Mama came to get me. Her face wild!

(in Mama's voice)
"What have you done Eva? What have you done to me?"

(in her own voice)
I killed us, Mama.

> *Beat.*

EVA
I don't like time on my own.

While Mama was living I took a week off every spring. Cleaned our apartment top to bottom. Well not her room. Not the room Jordan Fennel cleared out for her. Meant we each had a space of our own. I was not allowed in Mama's room. She kept it locked. The door was black with Storage written in red paint that flowed down like blood. It scared me a little. I might never have known what she was up to if I hadn't come home early one afternoon, sick as a dog.

I made my way to her room. Wanted her to know I was home and going to bed. Mama liked to know what was going on with me.

She had an old table in there and it was covered with tiny bits of wood, cloth. The room smelled of glue. She was building a dollhouse. So fine, so delicate.

There was a whole family. I mostly remember the father, standing outside the house, a briefcase tucked up under his arm. Coming home to the perfect life Mama built. She was hemming little curtains and talking away to Peg.

I never said a word. Just turned and went down to my room. I do that a lot. Walk away, not saying a word.

What good would it have done to tell Mama that Peg was too old to play with dolls? Except maybe with her own children.

Peg has at least one. I read that in the only letter of Beth Ann's I opened. It came years after the others. I thought it had been long enough...

I was a grandmother. Technically.

Beat.

EVA
Mama and I knew just how lonely technically can be.

The day she finished the dollhouse, Mama dropped dead in the middle of Melbourne Street. I saw her from the Sunnyside, turning from our apartment to the café and back again.

The same three gestures over and over. Right hand in her pocket searching, left hand to shield her eyes from the sun, then both hands to her mouth. Stroke can do that. Creates a loop and you go round and round like a merry-go-round until you don't.

Sofa

Five full circles before she dropped.

By the time the ambulance arrived all of Melbourne Street smelled of Mama's soup. She'd left a pot on the stove. No damage but smoke. Took years to get rid of the smell. Mama's chair still holds a little.

I even went to work on the day of her funeral. Didn't know anything else to do. Anywhere else to be.

Haven't taken any day but Sunday off since. And only Sunday like I said, because we're closed. Until the new owner. Bud. A real stickler for the rules. Made me take this week off.

Two days to clean. Two days to sit in Mama's chair in my uniform. Praying all the other waitresses would come down sick, leave Bud desperate. I'd be ready!

This morning I walked to the park. The merry-go-round was shut down. There was an 'out of order' sign hanging off my favourite horse. The black and white.

The kids were playing 'Mother May I?'

Mama may I? Mama may I?

I stayed most of the day in the park and when I got home I went up to Mama's room. Last time I was in there was to pick out her burying dress. I took her locket then. It holds the only picture of Peg and me. I don't know which one of us looks more frightened.

I couldn't bury it with Mama.

Today I took the dollhouse, carried it down to my room, cleared the top of my bureau with a sweep of my arm. I set it on the bureau, arranged the whole family in front of the house.

The baby was missing. It broke my heart. That one little sadness, that foot in the door...

I was so tired I thought I must be dying. So I put on a clean uniform and crawled into bed to wait.

I couldn't sleep.

Beat.

EVA
I woke a couple of hours ago, put my shoes on, pleased that I was

not going to spend eternity with everyone seeing my big toe out the hole in my pantyhose.

Then it came to me: Eva, you fool—thinking you're dying so you don't have to face living.

I am every bit as alive as I've ever been.

Peg will be here soon.

I'm going to do it this time. I'm going to hold my baby. I going to tell her Peg is for Pegasus. Peg. My out loud wanting.

I going to say I'm sorry.

I'm going to tell her about the box. She won't know how it smelled or how the purple taffeta was so dark it was almost black. Unless I tell her.

What would she make of what's inside? A photograph of a young man in uniform. He's been my Father ever since I stole the picture from Mama's drawer. My eyes are his eyes. But I don't know who he was, not really.

Mama's locket.

A child's pink sock.

And Malibu.

Eva repeats the next three gestures three times as she turns. She wipes her palms on her uniform, checks for her name tag, smooths her hair.

Blackout.

The end.

Thoughts on "Sunnyside Café"

Sherry Smith

The inner life of anyone is always something unexpected. What each of us is walking around with, for the most part, are hidden secrets, dreams, desires, hopes...you name it. Sometimes, in the company of trusted friends or family, parts of these secrets may be revealed.

In "Sunnyside Cafe", Eva puts her trust in the audience to share her most intimate and awkward moments that have brought her to this very special night where she anticipates the arrival of someone very important.

What I most appreciated about this script was the imagery and poetry of the language: the emotional impact of one item saved from a day in the laundromat, a pink sock that fits in the palm of her hand. I appreciate the slow and beautifully crafted unveiling of the events of the life before us that reveals to the audience who Eva has become, and why, in a brief 55 minutes. The lack of sentimentality allows the audience to tap into their own emotional response, and the carefully placed moments of humour help to open that door even more. It reminds us that even the briefest of encounters can change our lives for ever; sometimes for the best, sometimes for the worst.

It was overwhelming the response that this gentle, quiet, damaged character brought forth from the audience. It spoke deeply to many who came up to me afterwards weeping tears of gratitude. The character of Eva had allowed them safely to revisit their own stories, or the stories of those close to them. She had spoken the words out loud, giving their experiences validity. I had no idea this little play would have that kind of an impact.

The process of helping to develop this piece was also brought about by a director, Lee J. Campbell, who carefully nudged me along while not intruding on my exploration of Eva's inner monologue. Pam, the playwright, was VERY generous in accommodating rewrites that we suggested throughout the rehearsal process, fully trusting that we all wanted the best possible play at the end of the day. It was a very rare collaboration.

Sherry Smith played Eva in this play's premiere.

In the shadow of Sunnyside Café

I was adopted—a screaming reed of a failure-to-thrive baby. Twenty-eight years later I adopted my son whose birth weight was almost double my weight at five months.
   My son was never much concerned about his birth parents, but wondered often why they gave him up. What was wrong with him? I might have told him that I had those same feelings but I hadn't even identified them yet. Unlike my son, I thought about my birth mother almost every day.

> *Every Birthday*
> *I sit & wonder*
> *If somewhere*
> *A woman with eyes like mine*
> *Sits & wonders*
> *About the baby*
> *With eyes like hers.*
> *The baby she never held.*

And I feared her.

My real mother
comes for me,
clomping up the stairs
from a room in my house
that doesn't exist
until I sleep.

She is fat and ugly
old and stupid
cruel and unblest.

Pam Calabrese MacLean

> She calls
> for forgiveness.
>
> And the name she calls
> is mine,
> the one she gave me
> the day she gave me
> away.

I had no experience with giving a baby away: so, no forgiveness; no compassion; no understanding of my birth mother's decision.

As my sons grew I had to admit what I felt—abandonment. Slowly I realized that every woman, whether she gave birth, adopted, lost or denied a child, understands the weight of Eva's choice.

After trying for years to lift that weight and give Sunnyside Café a happy ending, I realized I was angry with my birth mother and I did not believe my she deserved any of those things.

After I came to grips with this, the ending practically wrote itself.

-PCM

Acknowledgements

I want to thank all the theatres that hosted productions of my plays, most especially the home team: Theatre Antigonish and Festival Antigonish.

Thanks to PARC for workshops, dramaturgy, readings and always the feeling of belonging in all ways. I had the great fortune to work with Jenny Munday many times in her years as PARC's Artistic Director (1997-2017). If not for Jenny's wisdom, knowledge, commitment and caring support I would not be the playwright I am today. RIP Jenny.

Mounting a play takes teamwork: lighting, sound, costumes, stage managing, props, directing, acting, audiencing. Thanks to all those folks who worked to bring the play out of my mind and onto the stage. I learned from every play, from every team member. Some lessons are forgotten but I seem to be hanging on to the stage manager's wisdom: righty tighty lefty loosey.

Thanks to Anne Simpson, who seems to always have a word for me. Thanks to a bevy of good friends sharing their time and so much more. Thanks to Pauline Liengme, my consummate Ida-Mae, my stalwart friend, with the patience to teach me so much. She even taught me to hug (properly!).

Thanks to Moose House Publications and its wonderful staff!

Thanks to my three sons who made me the tough broad I am.

And my lovely Ellie (Becca)!

Pam Calabrese MacLean

About the author

Pam Calabrese MacLean's writing for the stage includes

Her Father's Barn (Atlantic Fringe Festival (NS)) 2001; Festival Antigonish Late Night (NS) 2002; London Fringe (ON) 2005; Liverpool International Play Festival (NS) 2006; Uno Festival (BC) 2007; Mulgrave Theatre (NS) 2008; King's Theatre (NS) 2010);

Is it Wednesday? (King's Shorts (NS) 2010; Six Women International Playwriting Festival Colorado (US) 2011; Theatre Antigonish 2012;

Awake King's Shorts 2009; Theatre Antigonish 2012.

MacLean is also the author of two poetry books and two children's books. She lives in Nova Scotia.

www.ingramcontent.com/pod-product-compliance
Lightning Source LLC
Chambersburg PA
CBHW072329080526
44578CB00012B/584